MEDIEVAL GRAFFITI

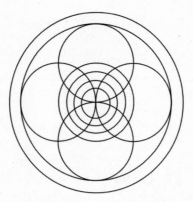

Typical compass-drawn consecration mark, Troston, Suffolk

C016065046

MEDIEVAL GRAFFITI

THE LOST VOICES OF ENGLAND'S CHURCHES

MATTHEW CHAMPION

EBURY
PRESS

1 3 5 7 9 10 8 6 4 2

Ebury Press, an imprint of Ebury Publishing,
20 Vauxhall Bridge Road,
London SW1V 2SA

Ebury Press is part of the Penguin Random House
group of companies whose addresses can be found at
global.penguinrandomhouse.com

Penguin
Random House
UK

First published in the United Kingdom by Ebury Press in 2015

www.eburypublishing.co.uk

A CIP catalogue record for this book is available from the British Library

ISBN: 9780091960414

Typeset by Palimpsest Book Production Limited, Falkirk, Stirlingshire

Printed and bound in Great Britain by Clays LTD, St Ives PLC

CONTENTS

A NOTE ON GEOGRAPHY

I am happy to admit to the reader that this book contains a great deal of bias towards sites in East Anglia and the south of England. While it is certainly true that East Anglia contains almost as many medieval churches as the rest of England taken as a whole, with more than 650 in the county of Norfolk alone, the real reason is far simpler. The recent church surveys from which many of the examples for this book are drawn began in Norfolk and the eastern counties, and that is where we have most information from. This does not, of course, mean that there aren't other fantastic examples of medieval graffiti to be found in churches all over Britain; there undoubtedly are. It's simply the case that nobody has really looked for them yet. They are all out there – just waiting to be discovered after centuries of hiding in the shadows . . .

FOREWORD

'You ignored the writing on the wall at your peril. Sometimes it was the city's way of telling you, if not what was on its bubbling mind, then at least what was in its creaking heart.'

Thud! – Terry Pratchett

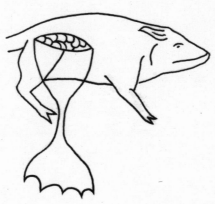

Pig and a chalice, Weybread, Suffolk

The chances are that if you read a newspaper story or magazine article that includes the words 'church' and 'graffiti' in the same sentence then the ending is unlikely to be a happy one. In the modern world, graffiti is widely regarded as both anti-social and destructive. It is seen as unacceptable behaviour that blights our streets, underpasses and railways with largely meaningless daubs of paint. The few artists who have moved beyond this level, to create stunning examples of contemporary street art, are largely the exception that proves the rule. Few people today could find any justification for leaving their mark scrawled across the stonework of a medieval church. Graffiti, to modern eyes, is nothing more than vandalism. Why, then, should the graffiti of the past be seen as any different? Why should the scratchings of our ancestors on the very fabric of their own parish churches be regarded as having any importance? Why should we devote time to discovering and recording ancient acts of anti-social destruction?

The simple answer is that ancient graffiti offers us something that most other areas of medieval and church studies cannot give us. It offers us a window into the medieval world, and the minds of those who created it. In particular, it offers us a rare glimpse of the lives of those who worshipped in the parish church; lives that otherwise have left almost no marks upon the world that they inhabited. Put simply, if you were to walk into one of the many hundreds of medieval churches that survive today, the chances are that you would come across a great many medieval survivals; carved bench-ends, colourful medieval wall paintings and shimmering stained glass. However, all these wonderful survivals tend largely to relate only to the parish elite. The coloured glass of the medieval church window and the dull brasses laid into marble upon the floor rarely carry images of peasants ploughing – they show instead the rich lords of the manor in all their finery; donor images kneeling before the Blessed Virgin herself or martial figures lying stiff in coat armour. Essentially, the inside of our churches are monuments to those who could afford to be memorialised in such a manner. Where, here, is the voice of those who worked the parish land, who carried the stones to build the church itself, and worshipped in this splendid monument to their betters?

The medieval parish church represented far more than just a place of religious worship, acting also as a focus for both community and social life within the village. It was a symbol of local pride, of church authority and religious salvation. Whatever its geographical location within the parish, the church building formed the central core of parish life. For the lower orders of the parish, life within the community began at its font, marriages took place within its porch and vigils for the dead were held beneath its roof. And yet, despite playing such a fundamental role in the rites of passage of countless generations of commoners, we still know very little of how these individuals, the vast majority of the medieval congregation, actually interacted with the church on a physical level. Their voice is largely silent. The voice of the commoners does turn up occasionally, in manor court records, legal documents and wills, but these documents are, in my opinion, rather atypical. They represent specific moments in time when those individuals came into contact with authority; the authority that ordered the medieval world. As such, they do not, and can not, truly reflect the attitudes and opinions of those people to their church, as either a building or an institution. Their voice has been muted by the constraints of authority.

It is in these areas of study, looking for the lost voices of the medieval village, that graffiti can play a crucial part. The images and texts that are inscribed into the very stones of the church building can often tell us far more about the medieval people who worshipped there than any amount of brightly coloured stained glass. Indeed, graffiti has the almost unique distinction of being able to be created by almost every class within the medieval parish. From the lord of the manor and parish priest to the lowliest commoner and peasant; all could, and did, leave their mark upon the church building. Far more than the idle scratching of bored choirboys, the medieval graffiti that we discover in churches today tells us about all aspects of the medieval world. It tells tales of grief and loss, of love and humour. At times, it speaks to us of religious devotion and fear of damnation. It carries names of long-dead children across the centuries, records happy days of pageants and celebrations.

In extreme cases, it tells us of events so dreadful and terrifying that those who were there to witness them believed that their own God had forsaken them, and that Judgement Day was coming fast upon them. In short, it tells us of life. Life and death in an English parish many hundreds of years ago.

CHAPTER ONE

IN THE BEGINNING

Medieval singer, Stoke-by-Clare, Suffolk

'The more closely we study the remains of early sacred art, the more frequently do we detect the smallest details have a meaning . . .'

The study of medieval church graffiti is not an entirely new phenomenon. Individual scholars and academics have been looking at these enigmatic inscriptions for several centuries. However, in most cases, these studies were based upon in-depth studies of specific churches. When a church was discovered to contain numerous examples of early graffiti, such as at St Mary's, Ashwell, Hertfordshire, it became the obvious focus for further research. In some cases, particularly in the nineteenth century, this work was undertaken by the parish priest or churchwardens, attempting to unravel the complex story of their own church and the community that once worshipped there. It was only in the middle of the twentieth century that the study of ancient church graffiti gained anything like respectability.

In 1967, Cambridge academic Violet Pritchard published the only full-length work that has ever been written on English church graffiti. Based on her research undertaken in the churches surrounding Cambridge, her work became the handbook for a generation of scholars and church enthusiasts. However, as Pritchard herself acknowledged, the book had many shortcomings. The most obvious of these was that she didn't have the resources to undertake the large-scale surveys needed. Written between the late 1950s and early 1960s Pritchard had no access to private transport and little official support or recognition for her work. As a result, she was forced to confine her surveys to churches within easy striking distance of her Cambridge base. Despite these limitations, Pritchard carried out a series of remarkable surveys that highlighted the massive quantities of medieval-graffiti inscriptions that were to be found in these churches. When her book was published, it was anticipated that this would be the first in a series of studies on the subject. This, however, wasn't to be the case.

Since the publication of Pritchard's book, the study of church-graffiti inscriptions has largely remained at the extreme fringes of research. A few individuals have carried on Pritchard's work but, like their nineteenth-century predecessors, this has largely been confined to studies of individual sites where graffiti has been found in quantity. The large-scale surveys of entire counties that Pritchard suggested were needed have not been carried out.

In many respects, this lack of study has been the result of the enigmatic nature of the graffiti itself. Unlike the unsightly and glaring painted daubs of much modern graffiti, the vast majority of medieval church graffiti is actually very difficult to see and record. In many cases, it is lightly etched into the stonework and, to the naked eye, is barely visible. Indeed, many inscriptions are only visible under particular lighting conditions and remain so only for as long as it takes to record them. While these inscriptions might be difficult to see and study today, that was not the case at the time they were created.

During the Middle Ages, the interior of the average parish church would have looked very different from the plain whitewashed walls that we see today. From the very earliest period, the inside of the medieval church was a place of vibrancy and colour. Just about every surface – the walls, pillars, arches and spandrels – would almost all have had painted decoration of some sort. Even the lower sections of the walls, which were usually free of the highly decorative painted schemes of saints and angels, would often have had a colourwash applied to the surface. In many churches, fragments of these colour schemes survive, allowing us to reconstruct how the inside of the church may have looked during the Middle Ages. At the church of St Mary the Virgin, Lakenheath, in Suffolk, the aisle piers were painted with unusual full-length figures in deep browns and reds. At Blakeney on the north Norfolk coast, we know that the piers of St Nicholas church were painted a deep red ochre, while a few miles inland, at Binham Priory, tiny fragments of pigment suggest that the piers were originally painted in alternating colours of red and black.

Inside these highly coloured medieval buildings, the graffiti inscriptions would have stood out far more clearly than they do today. In many cases, the graffiti inscriptions were actually carved through the bright pigments of the painted decoration to reveal the pale stone beneath. As a result, many of the graffiti inscriptions, far from being hidden away and difficult to see, would have been one of the most obvious things people entering the church would have noticed. At Blakeney, the dozens of examples of ship graffiti that cover the piers of the south arcade would have looked like a small white fleet sailing across a deep red-ochre sea.

The fact that very few of these highly visible graffiti inscriptions were defaced or destroyed also suggests that the medieval residents of the parish had a very different view of graffiti than we have today. In the case of the ship graffiti at Blakeney, we know that the images were created over a period of several hundred years. In addition, the individual ship images appear to respect the space of those that were created previously, deliberately avoiding any overlap with earlier inscriptions, until they were finally whitewashed over during the Reformation. As a result, we can be certain that these images, which would have covered several of the piers, were on show in the church for several centuries. During this time, they were not covered over or defaced, but were actually carefully added to over time. It must then be assumed that these images were respected by those who held power in the local church. They were, unlike almost all modern graffiti, both accepted and acceptable.

This idea is perhaps the key to understanding much of the medieval graffiti found in English churches. Modern perceptions of graffiti as something that is destructive and unacceptable simply cannot be applied to these medieval inscriptions. These early graffiti inscriptions had both meaning and function. In many cases, they were clearly devotional or votive in nature and a far cry from the random doodling of an alienated generation. They were the prayers, memorials, hopes and fears of the medieval parish.

CHAPTER TWO

RESEARCHING GRAFFITI

Medieval prayer inscription, Litcham, Norfolk

'In the first place – that every man of the trade may work at any work touching the trade, if he be perfectly skilled and knowing in the same'

London Regulations for the Trade of Masons of 1356

One of the major problems when researching medieval graffiti is the complete lack of comparable material and established research guidelines. Looking at medieval graffiti inscriptions is a relatively new area of study and few previous academics or researchers have examined it in any detail. While this certainly makes it a fascinating and exciting area to look at, the ground-breaking nature of the work means exactly that; the researcher has to start pretty much from scratch.

In normal circumstances, any new researcher would first look at all the previously published material written on his chosen subject, acquaint himself with the generally accepted theories and then begin to develop his own research framework – essentially, the questions that he or she were hoping to present answers for. However, when studying medieval graffiti, this context material just isn't there. The little already written on the subject tends to consist largely of site-specific studies of a single church, which do little to help understand the larger themes and bigger picture. A quick read of the published literature soon makes you feel as if you are using a magnifying glass to examine an elephant.

With such a lack of published research on the subject, the most obvious thing to do is to try to examine parallels within differing, but related, areas of study. In the case of medieval graffiti, the most obvious areas to look at are art history, architectural history, the study of medieval manuscripts and church archaeology. However, even here, there are problems. Much of the imagery used in medieval graffiti is fairly commonplace, crossing many boundaries between fields of research, but some of the more common imagery and symbols don't appear within mainstream studies. The disciplines of art history and medieval-manuscript study tend to depict only the mainstream orthodox view of the medieval world; the views put forward by the church authorities. Medieval graffiti and the imagery found scratched into our church walls tends to be at the other end of the spectrum. They represent the views and beliefs of the average medieval parishioner, and are as steeped in folklore and superstition as they are influenced by the teachings of holy mother church, so much of their symbolism and imagery simply isn't to be found within mainstream areas of medieval studies. Instead, the best (and sometimes only) place to find such comparable imagery is on the margins of medieval society.

In some cases, this is quite literally on the margins. While the study of medieval manuscripts might offer few insights on the imagery included in medieval graffiti, one very rewarding area of research has been the study of 'marginalia'. The marginalia of a medieval manuscript is the area outside the main body of the page and the text that contains most of the illuminated decoration. While the manuscript illustrator may have been confined to purely copy out and repeat passages of text when writing out the manuscript itself, particularly if it was a religious volume, he was usually given a fairly free hand when it came to the decoration of the page borders. As a result, many medieval manuscripts display a dazzling array of the weird and wonderful around their borders: jousting snails compete against wild men; foxes don priests' garments and preach from a pulpit before a crowd of geese; hunting dogs find themselves being hunted down by the rabbits and hares that should be their quarry. In effect, the borders of the medieval manuscript gave free rein to the illuminator's imagination and, as may be expected, they depict a world turned upside down. Rather than showing the world of the church fathers and their teachings, the illustrators depict a world of allegory, a world of folklore and a world of the fantastic. Their bright ink sketches put into pictures the world of the margins and images from the edge, and it is here that the same images and symbols that are seen in medieval graffiti are to be found.

In similar fashion, one of the other most useful areas of research into graffiti imagery has also been found on the margins of traditional medieval studies. Pilgrim badges and pilgrim souvenirs have been, like graffiti, a very specialised field of research in recent years. These cheap lead-cast badges were on sale at medieval shrines throughout Europe to the tens of thousands of pilgrims who, each year, made their way to the holiest sites of the Christian church in search of salvation, entertainment and redemption. They are recorded as far back as 1199, when the pope gave the authorities in Rome a monopoly on producing badges of St Peter and St Paul for sale to pilgrims, and they were subsequently made and sold in quite phenomenal numbers. Records show that the Swiss monastery of Einsiedeln managed to sell over 130,000 such badges in a single two-week period during 1466; making this trade a very significant source of revenue for many shrines.

In one sense, these badges were simply souvenirs for visitors to the holy shrines at sites such as Canterbury, Westminster Abbey and Walsingham, cheap baubles bought by Chaucer's pilgrims as proof of their journey and of their devotion. However, they are teeming with religious imagery and were often regarded as being holy in their own right. Records show that pilgrims would sometimes hang up their badges within the local parish church upon their return, leaving them as proof of their own journey and as a holy and miracle-working resource for their fellow parishioners. Many others have been found in rivers or streams, particularly at river crossings, suggesting that they were cast into the waters as offerings, or in thanksgiving for a safe journey. Early souvenirs took the form of small lead flasks or vials known as 'ampullae' that could be used to bring home holy water from the shrines. Such water was believed to have remarkable healing properties. However, as the easier-to-make badges gradually superseded the ampullae, those believed healing powers were transferred to the badges. One medieval account even tells of a woman who, when her own child was choking and near death, rushed to the church and pressed the pilgrim badges left there to the child's throat – after which it made an immediate recovery.

Pilgrim badges were, it appears, quite capable of the miraculous. These badges often depict episodes from the lives of the saints and, therefore, reflect the traditional teachings of the church. But they also include a mass of imagery that can be directly related to the folk beliefs of those undertaking such pilgrimages. These images are often to be seen on the back of ampullae, or in the borders and margins of traditional religious scenes, bringing together the accepted images of the medieval church with the everyday imagery of folk belief and superstition. Like the marginalia of the illuminated manuscripts, they go beyond the accepted imagery of the altarpiece, wall painting and stained-glass window. The symbols that they depict are not referred to within the orthodox religious texts of the period, or shaped into the corbels of our medieval cathedrals – but they are to be found scratched upon the walls of our medieval churches.

The fundamental problem with this, of course, is that very few people ever think to write down their reasons for believing in a superstition, let alone what many of their folk beliefs may be. Like throwing coins into a fountain or well, it is something that millions of people have done over many hundreds of years, but barely a handful have ever felt the need to write about it afterwards – and even if they did, then they are unlikely to leave behind a detailed explanation of their reasons for doing so. The same appears to be the case with medieval graffiti. Of all those thousands of individuals who left their inscriptions upon the walls, none seem to have felt the need to leave details of it in the written records – or if one or two did, then those records, like so many other medieval documents, have long since been lost. Rather than ascribing this to a selfish wish to frustrate future researchers, this appears to be due to our own lack of interest in recording the everyday or mundane. Even the most avid of diary writers is more likely to make mention of a party invitation received than the fact that they brushed their teeth after breakfast. And so it is with medieval graffiti. The tens of thousands of inscriptions still to be found across the walls of our churches are testament to the fact that it was most certainly commonplace, and the fact that the same symbols and images are to be found in churches across western Europe certainly suggests that it drew upon shared folk beliefs and ideas, and yet the documentary record is silent – leaving us scratching in the margins for meaning.

CHAPTER THREE

DATING GRAFFITI

Outline of a saint within a niche, Norwich Cathedral

'Lives of great men all remind us
We can make our lives sublime,
And, departing, leave behind us
Footprints on the sands of time'

H.W. Longfellow

The dating of the graffiti inscriptions we find in English parish churches is, in many cases, difficult to do with any degree of accuracy. While it is possible to ascribe a period, era or century to some individual inscriptions, many others remain enigmatic. In a large number of cases, the best that can be done is to describe an individual graffiti inscription as either pre- or post-Reformation. Even then, particularly with some of the simpler pictorial images, the borderline is distinctly hazy. The Reformation can be considered a major watershed, but it by no means marks a clear and immediate change in styles or content, and the hazy border is also quite a wide one. The Reformation does mark a period of abrupt change in many areas of church life and services, but at the level of personal beliefs, superstitions and piety, this change was slow; it happened, but it certainly didn't happen overnight. In terms of dating graffiti, this just adds another level of possible complication.

In most cases, the date ascribed to individual inscriptions is based upon a number of very imprecise factors. In the case of text inscriptions, the most useful method of dating is by the handwriting or script. Examples such as the short prayer on the aisle wall at Lakenheath, Suffolk, are of a typical late medieval style, while a number of the inscriptions located in the Abbey Church of St Alban have been identified as dating from the late thirteenth or early fourteenth centuries. However, such dating techniques also have the potential to be misleading. A number of highly decorative text inscriptions, such as that at Elsenham, Essex, appear to be either influenced by, or copied from, medieval manuscripts. Other examples have been identified at sites such as Blakeney in north Norfolk that would suggest that the highly decorated initial letters of medieval manuscripts may have been quite widely regarded as attractive patterns for graffiti. The problem is, of course, that the graffiti need not belong to the same date as the manuscript upon which it is based.

Sixteenth-century guild mark, Carlisle Cathedral

In a very few instances, text graffiti can be tied down to a quite precise time period and, in one or two cases, an actual recorded historical figure. At Wood Norton in Norfolk, the early-fifteenth-century porch is inscribed with the name 'Robert ffulsham'. The parish records show that a Robert of Foulsham was parish priest here until at least the year 1415 – after which he disappears and is presumed to have died. From the architectural style and construction details, it is likely that the church porch, into which the graffiti was etched, was constructed during the opening decades of the fifteenth century. As this appears to coincide with Robert Foulsham's time as parish priest, it is tempting to think that he inscribed his own name into the finished building as a record of his achievement. At St Mary's church, Troston, in Suffolk, a very clear and precise late fifteenth-century inscription on the tower arch records the name of 'Johes Abthorpe'. The Abthorpe, or Apthorpe, family held the manor of Troston throughout most of the fifteenth century, before finally leaving the area for good in about 1490. An individual called Johes (Johannes) or John Abthorpe is found as a witness on a number of important local wills throughout the 1460s and 1470s. Given that the inscription was created in very distinctive late-fifteenth-century lettering, it is likely that the witness to the wills was also the individual who created the inscription, and that it was therefore created at some point between 1460 and 1490. Though the dating of this inscription is reasonably reliable, which is unusual in itself, what we really don't know is exactly why the lord of the manor felt the need to inscribe his name into the stone of the church.

It can be possible to ascribe an inscription to a period of a few decades, but it is very occasionally actually possible to tie it down to an individual day of the year – even if the year itself is rather harder to pinpoint. The church of St Mary, Lidgate, in Suffolk, is unusual in a number of ways; the most obvious being that it was originally built within the outer bailey of a medieval castle. The castle itself is one of a number of such fortifications in East Anglia whose origins are distinctly unclear. It is likely that it was constructed either shortly after the Norman Conquest or during the turbulent years of the civil wars between King Stephen and the Empress Maud in the early twelfth century, but it appears so rarely in medieval records, and so little archaeological work has taken place at the site that nobody is, even today, quite sure. While the castle has long since gone, leaving only an impressive set of earthworks to show where it once stood, the church has both survived and thrived.

The church was heavily rebuilt in the fourteenth and fifteenth centuries, leaving little of the early church visible, and the wide aisles and finely finished octagonal piers appear to have been attractive sites for people to leave graffiti inscriptions. The result is a church that is literally crammed full of graffiti, among which are an unusually large number of text inscriptions that, from the style of text, are clearly medieval in origin. Among these, written in tiny lettering on the pillar by the south door, is an intriguing Latin inscription executed in a neat and practised hand. It translates simply as 'John Lydgate made/did this with licence on the day of St Simon and Jude' (28 October). Intriguingly, the quiet village of Lidgate was also the birthplace and family home of the famous late-medieval poet John Lydgate. A near contemporary of Geoffrey Chaucer, whom he greatly admired and referred to as his 'lode-star',

Lydgate spent most of his life as a monk in nearby Bury St Edmunds, a bare few miles from the village in which he was born. His output as a writer was prodigious, attracting the attention and patronage of the royal court and, in the years prior to his death in 1451, he was considered one of England's literary superstars.

Can we then assume that the inscription in Lidgate church, created on 28 October, was the work of John Lydgate the famous medieval poet? Well, the inscription was certainly created by someone very well used to the writing arts and well versed in Latin, as a literary monk of the great abbey at Bury St Edmunds would most certainly have been, and the style of text would suggest it dated from the opening decades of the fifteenth century. It is most certainly the right name, appearing in the right place, at the right time, by an individual with the right skills and experience. However, even then, we can never be 100 per cent certain. All we can say, without fear of overinterpreting the evidence, is that a John Lydgate made the inscription, on 28 October, at some point at the beginning of the fifteenth century. Considering that this particular graffiti text inscription appears fairly uncomplicated, it becomes clear that dating even the simplest early graffiti is never a straightforward task.

It is even harder to assign an actual date to non-text inscriptions with any degree of accuracy; in most cases ascribing something to a particular century, or era, may be the best that can be hoped for. Human figures may contain depictions of clothing that may help to date an inscription, such as those late-sixteenth- or early-seventeenth-century examples recently discovered at the Tudor House in Southampton. At the church of All Saints, Goxhill, Lincolnshire, the two figures of a kneeling lady and an armoured knight have both been dated to the fifteenth century from their costume, in particular the dress and head-dress of the lady; also, as the arcade upon which they are inscribed actually dates to the fifteenth century, in an earlier date would be an impossibility. In the Church of the Assumption of the Blessed Virgin Mary, in Harlton, Cambridgeshire, is a particularly well-executed inscription that shows the head and neck of a bearded man. The figure is clearly shown wearing a very distinct style of hat that was fashionable only in the first half of the fifteenth century and, as a result, the figure has been ascribed to this period. A very few examples have actually been ascribed an even more exact date, such as the figure of the halberdier found in All Saints church, in Leighton Buzzard, Bedfordshire, whose dress is so distinctive that it has been dated to between 1460 and 1480. In Norwich Cathedral, concealed beneath the shadows of the reliquary arch, is a full-length image of a robustly bearded Tudor figure, whose clothing contains enough accurate details – from the peascod-style doublet with its row of tiny buttons to the voluptuous panes of the trunk hose – to clearly date it to the 1570s or 1580s. Similarly, a figure in full Elizabethan costume on the walls of Thaxted church in Essex undoubtedly also belongs to the second half of the sixteenth century.

Other pictorial inscriptions can contain far fewer clues to the date of their creation. The very commonly discovered 'VV' symbols are found all over medieval churches, in stonework, timber and lead. In a medieval context, these are supposedly associated with the cult of the Virgin Mary, with some writers upon the subject claiming that they are found concentrated in churches with a Mary dedication, or in the region of the Lady chapel. However, the same symbol is also just as commonly recorded on fixtures and fittings that are clearly post-medieval in origin, upon everything from eighteenth-century pews to nineteenth-century replacement screens. Not only does this raise very serious questions as to the supposed association of the symbol with the Virgin, but it also throws into question the dating of examples found on medieval fixtures and fabric. Just because a symbol is carved into medieval material does not necessarily make it medieval in date.

Similar attempts have also been made to date various examples of ship graffiti, often found in coastal churches, by the style of ship or boat depicted. However, as the styles and designs of many craft, particularly those used inshore or in the fishing industry, actually remained virtually unchanged for many centuries, such methods are often not as useful as they might first appear. A small ship with a single mast and sail looks much like any other small ship with a single mast and sail. Only in a very few cases, such as that of the North Sea cog (a distinctive medieval trading vessel) recorded in the north Norfolk church of Cley Next The Sea, or the collection of ship graffiti inscribed into wet fourteenth-century plaster of Blackfriars Barn undercroft in Winchelsea, East Sussex, can more than a very general date be suggested. More general pictorial inscriptions may, in many cases, simply be impossible to date. If they lie beneath, or partially obscured by, the Reformation limewash, then a pre-Reformation date may be the best that can be hoped for.

At All Saints church, Litcham, in Norfolk, the mass of graffiti inscriptions that adorn the pillars have unusually been dated by the circumstances surrounding their creation rather than the inscriptions themselves. The church, like many other East Anglian churches, was a product of the 'great rebuilding' in the later Middle Ages, and records of this construction programme have survived to the present day. We know, for example, that the main arcades were actually constructed in the years immediately before 1412, with the church being rededicated on St Botolph's Day of that year. In similar vein, we also have records that indicate that the medieval wall paintings and decoration of the church were covered with limewash during the Reformation of Edward VI. Therefore, as a result of the documentary references that survive in the various archives, we can be pretty certain that the graffiti inscriptions on the pillars cannot pre-date 1412, and that those emerging from beneath the many layers of limewash were created prior to 1547. This information means that the inscriptions recorded at Litcham church must have been created in the 135-year period between 1412 and 1547. This method, of dating the inscriptions by the fabric into which they were originally inscribed, may not create the narrowest of possible margins but it does have the advantage of being supported by evidence from other sources, and, in one or two cases, this has been useful in adding weight to, and supporting, more precise dating of inscriptions.

One such example of the building fabric supporting further, more precise, dating of an inscription are the large architectural designs discovered at Binham Priory in north Norfolk. Here the numerous and large-scale inscriptions, some of which are over 2.4 metres tall, were carved into the twelfth-century stonework, but were located beneath a paint scheme that had previously been identified as dating to the fourteenth century. A suggested date of between the late twelfth century and early fourteenth century would, therefore, appear more than likely. However, the inscriptions themselves appeared to relate to the building of the nationally important west front of the priory – which took place in the decade prior to 1245 – and are likely to have been the master mason's original working drawings for the design. The fact that the inscriptions were located at a break in the building fabric, where one building phase had ended and another began, means that the dating of the fabric itself is crucial to supporting the suggested date for the inscription.

A very few inscriptions, far fewer than one would hope for, actually include a written date. The majority of these tend to be post-Reformation inscriptions. Indeed, it does appear that the actual year may have been of little importance to those who created these early inscriptions. Until the middle years of the sixteenth century, the inclusion of a date in graffiti inscriptions is an extreme rarity; and it does not become commonplace until the early years of the seventeenth century. This could be because the date was unimportant, or irrelevant, though it also coincides with the period when most individual's and legal documents dated events to the year of the reign of the current monarch, or 'regnal' year as it was known. From the middle of the sixteenth century, coincidentally coinciding with the Reformation, documents begin to move away from this system of dating and begin to more commonly use dating by calendar year, as we do today. In terms of graffiti inscriptions, the use of calendar-year dates has a major practical advantage. It is, after all, far easier to inscribe the date 1578 than is it to inscribe 'the twenty-first year of the reign of Elizabeth' or '21st Elizabeth'. In effect, the use of dates in medieval graffiti is sadly not something that you are likely to come across very often. The sudden appearance of dates in graffiti may also be linked to the Reformation in other, less obvious, ways. As most pre-Reformation inscriptions have devotional aspects, it might simply be that the date was considered unimportant. Why, indeed, would you need to date a prayer?

There are, of course, the odd exceptions to the rule. In cases such as plague graffiti (see below) and major parish events, the date does sometimes get included, but these are a rarity. A tiny inscription in St Mary's church in Ashwell is clearly dated to 1381; however, there is a large amount of debate as to what the inscription itself says. The noted church historian M.R. James believed the inscription to relate to the Peasants' Revolt of that year and reads: 'In AD 1381 was the insurrection of the common people'. However, early graffiti scholar and local historian Reginald Hine stated that it reads as: 'In the year of our Lord 1381, five ploughlands belonging to the church were exchanged'. Still other scholars have translated the same inscription as referring to the completion of the church rebuilding after the great storm of 1361, and a record stating that in that year the church's own quarry was finally worked out. It would therefore appear that, even when clear dates are present, understanding some graffiti inscriptions is still far from straightforward.

CHAPTER FOUR

PROTECTING THE SPIRIT: RITUALISTIC GRAFFITI

A typical compass-drawn 'Hexfoil' or 'Daisy Wheel' design

'Superstitious ritual often survived the religious beliefs that gave birth to it, and was reinterpreted in the light of current beliefs . . .'

R. Merrifield, The Archaeology of Ritual and Magic

Perhaps the most common single type of early inscription recorded in English medieval parish churches is that which is regarded as 'apotropaic' graffiti. Commonly known as 'ritual protection marks', or even 'witch marks', an apotropaic image or symbol is a marking that is thought to create 'protection' for the individual that created it – or for the area or object into which it was inscribed. Derived from the Greek *apotropaios*, meaning to 'turn away evil', the term apotropaic has come to refer to all symbols of protection. This protection could take many forms. At its most simple level it can be thought of as something that was thought to bring good luck while warding off bad luck, or the 'evil eye'. However, the concept isn't quite so straightforward. At its most fundamental level it is a symbol that brings general good fortune, in much the same way that picking a four-leaf clover might still be regarded. At a more complex level it was regarded as offering protection to a particular object or individual from a specific threat or collection of threats.

Until very recently it was believed that the vast majority of these types of markings were to be found in domestic and agricultural buildings, and dated usually to the sixteenth, seventeenth and eighteenth centuries; any quick examination of the beams above fireplaces or around doorways in old houses will often bring some to light. However, this was largely because these later buildings have been examined in far greater detail – and survived in far greater numbers – than their medieval counterparts. There was even a suggestion that when these markings were discovered in churches, they, too, had been created in the seventeenth and eighteenth centuries and inscribed into medieval stonework. However, recent research has shown that this isn't the case.

The expansion in the study of church graffiti has meant that many, many more of these inscriptions are now being recorded – thousands more – and a significant number have come from securely dated medieval contexts. They have been recorded in the demolition rubble from the great medieval pilgrimage centres such as Walsingham Priory, and among the stones recovered from the remains of the cloisters of Whitefriars in Canterbury. More intriguingly, they have also been found beneath medieval pigment in Norwich Cathedral and beneath Reformation limewash at All Saints, Litcham in Norfolk. It appears clear that though these symbols continued in use in domestic buildings through to the eighteenth or even nineteenth centuries, they were also common features of medieval churches. They are also to be found in some of the surviving medieval domestic buildings, although the scarcity of such buildings and the number of renovations they will undoubtedly have been subjected to means it is difficult to be sure how widespread this practice was.

While the temptation is to assume that such symbols were associated with 'superstitious' or even 'magical' beliefs, and are therefore fundamentally irrational and outside of the traditional beliefs and services of the church, it must be remembered that we are viewing the practice from a wholly modern perspective. The medieval church, particularly at the parish level, was a place where magic and ritual were central to the services of the Church. From the Transubstantiation of the Latin Mass, where the blessed wine and bread were believed to physically transform into the blood and body of Christ, to the blessing of the plough to ensure good harvests, or the ringing of church bells to ward off lightning, the medieval church encouraged and fostered a belief in the protective power of physical symbols. As we've already heard, a leaden 'pilgrim badge', acquired by a pilgrim for a few pence from a street trader at one of England's many shrines, could be used as a potent talisman to help the sick. The viewing of an image of St Christopher through an open church doorway would protect the individual from sudden or unexpected death for the length of the day. Such beliefs were commonplace throughout much of the Middle Ages and had their basis in established and accepted practice rather than scripture and professed doctrine. Everyone appears to have participated in these activities, and have believed that they had at least some power, but you most certainly won't find them referred to in the church documents of the time.

It is, therefore, a simple step in terms of belief to understand the accepted power of these apotropaic symbols. Indeed, the difference between established church practice and superstitious magic would only have been the difference between what was seen as doctrinally legitimate and that which was illegitimate. For the congregation of the medieval parish, the dividing line between the two, if such a thing existed, was very blurred indeed. The systems of belief, and the hoped-for results of the action of creating these marks, were all but identical – and such beliefs shifted and evolved over time. In 1450, it was accepted and expected that churchgoers would pray to images of the saints to ask them to intercede on their behalf. In 1550, the images had been destroyed and such prayers were condemned. However, in the minds of the parishioners, those individuals who lived, worked and sought everlasting salvation within the medieval parish, the beliefs that had led to the creation of such apotropaic markings persisted. The manner in which they were created might alter over time, and the places into which they were inscribed might change, but the fundamental beliefs that lay behind them remained long after the statues, stained glass and wall paintings had been scoured from the church. Given the sheer quantity and widespread distribution of these markings in English churches, it would appear that they were as much a part of the everyday experience of the church as the Mass, the blessing of newborn children or intercessions for the dead.

There are three main motifs that form the central group of these apotropaic markings found among medieval-church graffiti; the compass-drawn design, the pentangle and the 'VV' symbol. While there are many other symbols that were, and are, considered to be 'protective', these three symbols, and their many, many variants, appear time and time again. While the majority of these symbols are found inscribed into the stone fabric, they can also be discovered inscribed into the other fixtures and fittings of the medieval church. In most cases, this means wood. The same symbols that are found etched into the stone walls are also found scribed into bench-ends, on the backs of rood screens or carved into the planking of the parish chest. Less commonly, these same symbols can be found etched into the lead linings of fonts or the surface of medieval wall paintings. Most of these symbols – with the exception of the 'VV' markings – have one thing in common, and that is that they are all made in the form of an 'endless line'. It is believed that this idea that endless lines were useful for protection from evil, stretches way back beyond the Christian period, and echoes of it can be found in the stories of sacred knots and puzzles, such as the tale of the Gordian knot, the mandala and, perhaps more significantly, in the story of Solomon's knot. One of the ideas behind the protective power of these endless knots is that demons, the 'evil eye', call it what you will, are attracted to lines and, if they come across one, will follow it to its end. Therefore, the power of the endless knot is that once the evil begins to follow the line it will never come to an end, thereby trapping itself within the symbol.

Unusual eight-petalled compass-drawn design, Marsham, Norfolk

Between them, these symbols represent a level of folk belief that permeated the whole of medieval society, an aspect of religious belief that, taken in context, was as central to the everyday lives of the medieval commoner as the next meal, the next harvest and the next year. They are the physical remains of something that we may find a little alien today; a little backward and superstitious but, at the time, they were considered everyday reactions to a common and well-recognised threat. The world was a place full of dangers, both physical and spiritual, and these markings were made simply as a way to make that world a safer, less hostile place; the front line in the defence of the soul.

CHAPTER FIVE

COMPASS-
DRAWN
DESIGNS

Elaborate compass-drawn Hexfoil, Norwich Cathedral

'*Five for the symbols at your door . . .*'

Green grow the rushes oh *(Traditional folksong)*

The chances are that any medieval church you go into that contains early graffiti will contain at least one compass-drawn design – and most usually, more. They are among the most common types of graffiti and certainly one of the most-used of the symbols loosely termed as apotropaic, or ritual protection marks. Certain churches, such as Brisley in Norfolk or Lanercost Priory in Cumbria, have been found to contain several dozen examples. Even churches that contain no great quantity of graffiti, such as St Mary's, Lamberhurst in the Weald of Kent, are still found to have multiple examples of these compass-drawn designs. Though we now believe most of the designs are ritual protection marks, that has not always been the case. Until very recently, debate still raged in certain circles as to exactly who created these symbols, and why.

These marks are so common in many churches that they have not escaped the notice of resident vicars, churchwardens and historians in recent centuries – all of whom tended to come up with theories as to why they were there. One of the earliest theories dates back to the very early years of the twentieth century and was published by a Cambridge-based academic, T.D. Atkinson. Atkinson was a well-respected and widely published architectural historian, well known for undertaking his own fieldwork, rather than relying upon the observations of others. Several of his architectural works were the standard books upon the subject until very recently. In the late nineteenth century, Atkinson was one of the very few researchers looking at, among other things, the specialist field of church 'consecration crosses'.

Today, consecration crosses are not widely known about except among those who study medieval churches. When any medieval church was first built, it would have to undergo the ceremony of consecration by the local bishop. This would involve the bishop anointing the building with holy oil, traditionally twelve times inside and twelve times outside. On the inside of the church, and sometimes upon the outside, too, the place where the holy oil was applied to the wall would then be marked with a painted or carved cross. Today, many of these crosses still survive within our churches, but few churches have more than one or two examples and, unless they have been repainted, they are invariably in poor condition. Some of these consecration crosses were very elaborate, such as the foliage-surrounded examples from Bale in north Norfolk. However, it was far more typical for the crosses to be fairly simple compass-drawn crosses within a circle; typical examples can be seen at Thompson in Norfolk, St Mary's in Fairford, Gloucestershire, at Inglesham in Wiltshire, Radnage in Buckinghamshire, and Lamberhurst. In these cases, the design was first marked into the stonework or plaster using a large pair of compasses or dividers before painting. At some sites, such as Westerham in Kent, the markings can still be made out high up on the pillars of the arcades, despite the fact that no trace of pigment survives. At other sites, such as Great Walsingham in Norfolk, the surviving consecration cross clearly shows further compass-drawn marks beneath the pigment, suggesting that the current cross actually replaced a far earlier example.

Atkinson was studying half a dozen sites around Cambridge where consecration crosses were known to still exist, including one former church at Isleham that was at the time used as a barn. What he noticed was at each of these sites the buildings also contained many examples of compass-drawn marks other than the consecration crosses. Putting two and two together, Atkinson came to the conclusion that the compass-drawn designs he was discovering were actually directly related to the crosses themselves. Oddly enough, Atkinson's theory, published in a local archaeological journal, has actually had a far greater impact and longevity than even he would have imagined, and is still being repeated today. To be fair to Atkinson, his theory does have a number of factors to support it, and there are a small number of compass-drawn designs that are undoubtedly the remnants of now-lost consecration crosses. At both Troston in Suffolk and Ludham in Norfolk, identical elaborate compass-drawn designs are to be found inscribed into either side of the tower arch – a traditional site for consecration crosses to be placed – which may well be the fragmented outlines cut into the stonework prior to the originals being painted. In addition, not all surviving consecration crosses are shown as actual crosses; a number are shown as either six-pointed stars, such as at Carleton Rode in Norfolk, or the six-petalled design known as a 'daisy wheel' that appears so often among compass-drawn designs, such as at the church of St Mary the Virgin, Cerne Abbas in Dorset.

Compass-drawn design, Wiveton, Norfolk

Despite this, Atkinson's theory really presents too many problems when compared to the evidence to explain the origins of most of the compass-drawn designs. First, consecration crosses tend to be quite large designs – in some cases up to almost a metre across – while the vast majority of inscribed compass-drawn designs tend to be far smaller, sometimes only two or three centimetres across. In addition, consecration crosses tended to be placed on the stonework or wall plaster in particular positions, such as at each side of the chancel arch and each side of the tower arch. Compass-drawn graffiti tends to follow no such patterns, being found all over the church and cut into the stonework, the plaster on the walls, the timber of the church pews, the lead lining of the font, or even the font itself. Then there is the sheer quantity of compass-drawn graffiti that is being recorded. Each church should have only a dozen consecration crosses located inside the building. Even if we allow for the occasional re-consecration of a church – which usually took place after major buildings works had been undertaken or if the church had been defiled in some manner (such as having blood shed upon the premises) – so that multiple consecration crosses may be present, this still cannot account for churches where dozens of compass-drawn designs are found in one area, such as on the rear of the chancel arch at Brisley church in Norfolk. In short, there are simply too many of the compass-drawn designs, of the wrong size and in the wrong places, for more than a handful of the recorded examples to have been associated with the sites of consecration crosses.

A second theory as to the origins of these often beautiful designs is one that still finds favour among a number of architectural historians, despite the wealth of evidence to the contrary – that all of these inscriptions were actually created by the medieval masons who built the churches and cathedrals into which they are inscribed. It has been argued that the people most likely to have access to the tools needed to create these designs, being either dividers or compasses, were the master masons. Indeed, the large-scale compass was so widely used by masons that, along with the right-angle square, it became a symbol almost synonymous with the craft itself. Medieval masons are depicted in manuscripts holding just such a pair of compasses and squares, their tombs were embellished with the motif and their monumental brasses are etched with the design. The compass and square are so deeply associated with the mason's craft that they are still used as the symbol for the modern Masonic order. With compasses or dividers being fairly rare items in terms of the archaeological record, the idea that all the compass-drawn motifs were created by masons, who actually had access to the tools needed, almost seems logical.

But why would these medieval masons be so obsessed with inscribing the walls of our churches with intricate compass-drawn designs? What drove them to inscribe quite literally thousands of these designs into the stone, wood and lead fabric of the churches they were working on? The simple answer, we are asked to believe, is that they were using these designs to train their apprentices in the basics of geometry. Like Atkinson's theory before it, the idea is an attractive one. For anyone with a love of geometry, these simple compass-drawn designs are some-thing of a magic symbol in their own right. However, before you can truly appreciate the 'magic', you must understand exactly how these designs are made. First, you must draw your simple circle with your pair of compasses and then, without moving the arms of your compass, you place the point upon the outside circle and draw an arc. You then move the point of the compass to where the arc intersects the outer circle – and draw another arc, repeating until you have a complete six-petal design, so beloved of schoolchildren down the ages. It is at this point that the real geometric magic begins. If you now join up all the points of the petals, you will find that you have a perfect hexagon. If you join up the points of only every second petal, you will create the perfect equilateral triangle. If you then join up the points of the remaining three petals, you will find that, in the centre of the design, you have a perfect scaled hexagon . . . and so it goes on. From that one simple compass-drawn circle, you can create hexagons, equilateral triangles, right-angled triangles, diamonds and perfectly proportioned rectangles. In short, from that one compass-drawn circle, you can derive all the basic geometric knowledge needed to build a church or cathedral.

Large and elaborate compass-drawn design, Sedgeford, Norfolk

Elaborate multiple compass-drawn 'Hexfoil' design, Ludham, Norfolk

There are, of course, some compass-drawn designs found in churches that were the work of masons. Leaving aside the clearly architectural designs, most probably created as working drawings for actual building projects, there are also a few geometric constructions that could only have been created by masons. Among the most obvious of these are a number of spiral designs, obviously created with a compass, with examples found on Duke Humphrey's monument in St Albans Cathedral and at the remote church of Bedingham in Norfolk. More extensive designs are to be found at Belaugh church in the Norfolk Broads, where the pillars of the arcade are absolutely covered in many dozens of compass-drawn designs. Here can be seen elaborate quatrefoil and trefoil geometric constructions that are clearly the work of a mason or similar craftsman, working out their designs with a mathematical exactitude upon the stones of the church itself.

Despite the mathematically attractive nature of the idea that all these compass-drawn designs actually represent hard-working master masons attempting to teach their apprentices the very basic skills needed in their craft, such a theory also has a number of quite fundamental problems. As with Atkinson's theory, the size of the designs is an issue. Mason's dividers tend to be large-scale items, intended for drawing out architectural designs that could be later used for stone-cutting templates, whereas most of the compass-drawn designs found in churches tend to be small scale, often no more than ten centimetres across. In addition, from a number of surviving manuscripts and architectural treatises, it is known that masons could and did use a wide variety of techniques and designs to create their geometric constructs, and invariably taught these also to their apprentices – but none of these designs are to be found inscribed into our church walls. Last, and perhaps most tellingly, there is the sheer quantity of these designs that are being recorded; there are too many of them for masons to have been solely responsible for their creation. For them to all be the work of masons, we would either have to accept that there were far more masons wandering the highways and byways of medieval England than the evidence suggests, or that they had some very stupid apprentices who required being shown the same simple design time after time after time. As with Atkinson's theory before it, there are just too many of these designs, created at the wrong scale and in the wrong places, for any more than a handful of them to have been created by masons.

Even if we accept that most of these compass-drawn markings were not associated with consecration crosses, and were not the work of medieval masons, why then are we so sure that the majority of these designs are ritual protection markings? Well, the answer is actually far more straightforward than most people might imagine. Quite simply, we are discovering many, many hundreds of these markings in distinct concentrations alongside other symbols that are already recognised as ritual protection marks. At some sites, such as Edgefield in Norfolk, the compass-drawn design has actually been incorporated into another symbol; in this case, the well-recognised symbol for the Trinity. At Sawston in Cambridgeshire, the Trinity symbol itself has been constructed in the exact same manner as a hexfoil. The term 'hexfoil' is often used to describe these designs, being derived from a mixture of the geometrically correct term sexfoil and the widely used term 'hex sign', the name given to the symbol by the Pennsylvania Dutch immigrants who used it to protect their barns and outbuildings. At other sites, such as Swannington in Norfolk and Ashwell, masses of ritual protection marks are found in close proximity, with heavy concentrations, including compass-drawn designs, located around areas within the church that were deemed to be particularly spiritually significant. Indeed, in some cases, it is actually these concentrations of graffiti that can indicate that these places, which might now be devoid of any specific spiritual focus, were once the sites of side altars, guild chapels or devotional imagery.

If we accept that the majority of these markings are ritual protection marks, designed to ward off the 'evil eye', then we are still left with a number of fascinating questions: Exactly who made these markings? Why were they carving them into the walls of our churches? How were they made? The last of these questions, as to how these sometimes highly complex designs were created, is perhaps superficially the most intriguing. The reason for this is that dividers or compasses are really quite rare discoveries in the archaeological record, meaning that there would not have been very many of them about. To put it into context, the Museum of London undertook a whole series of excavations along the Thames embankment in the 1970s and 1980s, and these discovered many tens of thousands of artefacts from medieval London. The sites that they were examining were areas where, every fifty years or so, a new timber river wall had been built, each one slightly further on to the foreshore, narrowing and controlling the river. The area behind each of these new river walls was then infilled with the rubbish of the medieval city. The result was an archaeologist's treasure trove. The tens of thousands of artefacts, all of which could be fairly accurately dated, offered a cross-section of London life at the time. What was really noticeable was the number of iron items that were recovered, including hundreds of knives and dozens of pairs of scissors and shears. However, in all of the excavations, and among all those thousands of artefacts, there was only one set of dividers. The same is true of excavations elsewhere across the country, at sites such as Norwich and York, where many dozens of knives and general iron items are recovered, but almost no sets of dividers or compasses.

This does actually leave us with a little bit of a problem with regard to these ritual protection marks. Are we to believe that all these thousands of designs were created using a tool that was actually extremely rare and only regularly used by stonemasons and carpenters? Surely the tool that created these designs needs to have been far more common, and far more accessible to everyone throughout medieval society, than the rarely found dividers? For one possible answer, we must look more closely at the finds from the excavations in London, where the largest single type of iron tool recovered was, by far and away, knives. Most of these were small domestic knives that just about everyone would have carried about their person, and were most probably used first and foremost for eating. Ranging from rather crude wooden-handled ones to the ornate and highly decorative, they are also quite likely to be the tool that was used to create many examples of our medieval church graffiti. After the knives the most common type of tool discovered, not just in London but elsewhere, are scissors and shears. The shears, forged from a single piece of iron, are made to form two opposed cutting blades attached by a curved spring. Such shears came in all shapes and sizes, the larger ones being used for rough cutting work such as sheep shearing, with smaller and more delicate versions used for everyday chores such as needlework. Indeed, these shears appear in numerous medieval manuscript illustrations, often shown as hanging from women's belts or in scenes of domestic life; they are also absolutely perfect for creating many of the compass-drawn designs found in our parish churches. In many respects, these small shears are slightly more practical for making these designs than compasses or dividers, with the fixed arms making it far harder to make a mistake. These would most certainly have been easily accessible to just about everyone in society; most particularly the women. This possible association of women with some of these compass-drawn designs may well be reinforced by evidence that has emerged from a number of churches concerning the distribution patterns of these markings.

The origins of the compass-drawn circle as a ritual protection mark are unclear. It may well have its origins in Roman architectural decoration, with compass-drawn designs featuring as common window-head decorations at a number of surviving Roman British sites such as Housesteads fort on Hadrian's Wall, but it is unclear how this may relate to the designs found within medieval churches. What is clear is that by the late eleventh century these compass-drawn designs had begun to be a regular feature of church decoration, and this may well answer the question of exactly who created these designs and why they made them. In the southwest of England, they were most obviously associated with fonts, and a number of finely carved examples are still to be found at churches such as Buckland-in-the-Moor and Combeinteignhead, where the daisy wheel forms the central theme to the decorative scheme of both font bowl and its support. A group of four or five eleventh-century fonts from west Norfolk, all possibly created by the same craftsman, also share the same motif as an integral part of their decoration. The finest of these superbly carved fonts, from Sculthorpe and Toftrees, have the simple daisy wheel shown quite prominently, but also feature other recognised apotropaic symbols as well. A few miles away, at Reymerston in central Norfolk, a fragment of an early-Norman font is preserved in the village church, which also shows that the daisy-wheel design was a central part of its decorative scheme, and similar examples are to be found in St Andrew's church, Bredwardine in Herefordshire and at Egleton in Rutland.

The association of compass-drawn motifs with fonts would suggest that the medieval church and congregation assumed that there was a need for protection for the newborn child from evil influences, displaying an understandable logic that is often far from clear in many of the other areas in which these symbols are to be found. However, while the formal decoration of the fonts is only indirectly linked to the phenomena of graffiti inscriptions, a number of East Anglian churches have shown distribution patterns of compass-drawn imagery that may well suggest a continued association with the church font and areas immediately surrounding them.

Swannington church in Norfolk contains a very large collection of early graffiti inscriptions spread throughout the entire church and includes a large number of complex compass-drawn designs. But all of these, almost without exception, are located between the first two piers of the north arcade – the probable original location of the church font. Similarly, at another Norfolk church, St Andrew's at Bedingham, the compass-drawn motifs are located on the most easterly pier of the south arcade, facing the side altar in an area once used as a separate chapel, and between the two most westerly piers of the north arcade – again the likely original position of the font. Similar patterns of distribution have been recognised in other East Anglian churches, such as Lidgate in Suffolk, where a mass of ritual protection marks, including compass-drawn designs, are to be found facing the area at the west end of the north aisle. At the church of St Barnabas church in Great Tey, Essex, it is the font itself that is covered in such markings, inscribed deeply into almost any remotely flat surface.

The apparent link between the area containing the font and the distribution patterns of the compass-drawn designs is an intriguing one that raises a number of issues. The perceived need for ritual protection marks around areas where an unbaptised – and therefore, vulnerable – infant was to be found would appear relatively straightforward, with clear links to the act of baptism itself. As the child is welcomed into the church, the holy water drives away any evil spirits to be found in the baby, while the ritual protection markings offer heightened levels of protection, and could act as a trap for the spirits either driven out of, or drawn towards, the vulnerable infant.

Although such beliefs may seem a little alien to modern minds, the superstitions surrounding baptism remain almost as strong today. In some churches, it is still a tradition that the north door, sometimes known as the 'Devils Door' after the association between evil and the north side of the churchyard, is left ajar during the ceremony, to allow the evil to exit the building unhindered. In a few churches, particularly in the south of England, it is still possible to see small window-like openings set into the north side of the church that are only opened during the baptism service – again, to allow the evil within the unbaptized child to leave the church by the quickest possible route.

With baptism regarded as one of the key seven sacraments of the church, its importance within the local church community would have appeared, in a number of churches, at least, to have led to the creation of an additional ritualised level of protection – hence the proliferation of the symbols. It is also rather intriguing to note that these same distribution patterns of ritual protection marks, clustering near or around the font, are found all over the country, and into mainland Europe as well, suggesting that these beliefs weren't only the product of a few local people, but were widespread throughout the Christian west. Parents, perhaps, of newborn babies all across the Christian world had a knowledge and understanding of this practice, despite the fact that it appears never to have been written about. In addition, the link between the location of these compass-drawn designs and baptism may well suggest clear gender bias in their creation. The female association with the act of childbirth and subsequent baptism leads to the intriguing possibility that these designs around the font may have been created largely by women using the small iron shears that many of them would have owned or had common access to.

While the link between these markings and fonts or baptism is certainly suggestive, it cannot possibly account for more than a small percentage of the compass-drawn designs that have been recorded. It must also be remembered that, due to numerous repairs and renovations in a typical church, we are only ever looking at a partial distribution pattern, and we may, therefore, be missing many other sites like Swannington and Lidgate. There are also many more sites where something else is clearly going on. Concentrations of these marks, particularly the hexfoil or daisy-wheel designs, are to be found all over medieval churches, and they clearly cannot all relate to locations where the font once was. In some cases, such concentrations may simply relate to an area that was, at one time, a side altar or guild altar. With the original feature probably removed at the time of the Reformation, when many such 'superstitious' things were outlawed, the concentration of graffiti may indeed be the only physical indication that there was ever anything important taking place in that part of the church. However, the fact that such concentrations do occur, suggests that these markings had evolved from being seen as adding layers of protection only to the font and were being be regarded as having more general protective attributes. They had transformed from something that offered a very particular level of protection in very specific circumstances to being all-encompassing ritual protection marks.

The fact that these symbols, most particularly the hexfoil, came to be seen as a general mark of spiritual protection is nowhere better demonstrated than by looking at the other objects within the parish church to which it was applied; most notably, the parish chest. There are many absolutely superb examples of medieval parish chests to be found all over England, and they can vary in quality almost as much as they can vary in size. At St Mary's church in Kempley, Gloucestershire, is a chest that appears to have been crudely carved from a single block of wood before being bound in rough bands of iron, while at Malpas in Cheshire, the long parish chest is decorated with the most intricate iron scrollwork that dates back to the thirteenth or fourteenth century. At Rainham in Kent can be found a beautifully carved parish chest, dating back to the fourteenth century, that ranks among the very finest pieces of medieval furniture to survive in any English church.

The parish chest can be thought of as the administrative centre of the medieval parish. It was within the parish chest that the 'treasures' and documents of the medieval church would have been stored. Here would be kept the expensive vestments and regalia of chalices, censers and ornate crosses used during the services, as well as the parish records, deeds and documents and, upon occasion, parish funds in the form of gold and silver coins. The chest was, in effect, the parish strongbox that stored both its civil and religious items of value and, as such, access to the chest was strictly controlled. As you will still see on most surviving parish chests, they were usually secured with not one but three locks or padlocks. Each lock would be opened by a separate key, which were each held by the two churchwardens and the parish priest, meaning that the chest could only be opened in the presence of all three, ensuring that none of them could act alone or without the consent of the others.

The level of protection afforded to these parish chests went far beyond the stout oak, iron bands and strong locks. The physical security against theft and tampering may have deterred thieves from trying their luck with the parish valuables, but they would have been ineffective against the evil spirits that may have sought to break into the parish chest. The obvious and seemingly logical reaction to this threat was to add a layer of spiritual protection to the physical protection already in place and, for this, the medieval community turned to ritual protection marks. Close examination of dozens of surviving medieval parish chests have shown that many of them were very deliberately carved, incised and decorated with ritual protection marks; most usually, the compass-drawn hexfoil. At Hindringham in Norfolk, the elegantly carved late-medieval chest is quite literally covered in inscribed and painted hexfoils, set in vertical lines that appear to have formed part of a formal decorative scheme. A few miles away at South Acre, the carved medieval chest in the north aisle has hexfoils shown prominently among the carved decoration, where they sit among ciphers to the Virgin Mary and other religious imagery. In some cases, as at Field Dalling church, also in

Norfolk, the compass-drawn designs have been etched into the lid in a more haphazard manner; while at St Michael's church in Hernhill, Kent, the solidly constructed chest, again carved from a single tree trunk, still shows faint signs of compass-drawn designs in several areas.

From this, it becomes apparent that these compass-drawn designs, and particularly the hexfoil and all its many variations, were seen as offering a level of spiritual protection to both places and objects. They sat not outside the teachings of the church, but were a physical reflection of those beliefs that the church taught to the people of medieval England. Evil was abroad, it was all around them, biding its time and waiting for even the smallest opportunity to damage their souls and, ultimately, claim them for the Devil. While the church offered its own form of protection, via prayer, ritual and ceremony, the parish could augment and enhance that with defences of its own. These compass-drawn designs were one aspect of that defence. Not simply a reflection of silly superstition, built more from tradition than true belief, but a direct attempt to combat the forces of evil and make the medieval parish a safer place for one and all.

CHAPTER SIX

THE DEMONS ON THE WALL: PENTANGLES

Late medieval 'Demon' inscription, Troston, Suffolk

'It is a symbol that Solomon designed long ago
As an emblem of fidelity, and justly so'

Sir Gawain and the Green Knight, *C14th, Anon.*

The five-pointed star, or pentangle, is most certainly one of the less prolific ritual protection marks found in medieval churches. Compared to the compass-drawn motifs, it is relatively rare, appearing in only a few dozen or so Norfolk churches surveyed to date, and is just as rare further afield. However, it appears in sufficient quantities and in enough diverse locations for it to be regarded as an apotropaic marking. More interestingly, a number of examples have been recorded in very specific locations as to be able to suggest that the pentangle was more than just a general 'witch mark' designed to ward off evil, but that it actually had a distinct and identifiable function.

The pentangle is an extremely ancient symbol whose use has been recorded as far back as 3000BC, where it formed part of the ancient Sumerian pictogram language. To the Greeks, it was regarded as a symbol of mathematical purity or perfection, in similar manner to the geometric perfection of the daisy wheel or hexfoil. Since the Reformation, the symbol has become associated with the magical arts and, in more recent centuries, it has become particularly associated with Wiccan practises and Victorian concepts of 'black magic'. Indeed, its discovery in medieval churches has in the past few decades caused disquiet among local church authorities, who believe it to be a sign of improper practices taking place in the church building. However, during the Middle Ages, it is clear that this symbol was regarded as a specifically Christian symbol with no 'evil' connotations and, more specifically, was seen as a symbol of protection. Intriguingly, it is also one of the very few ritual protection marks for which we have any documentary evidence to support its supposed meaning and function.

In the late fourteenth century, an unknown poet, most probably from north-western England, wrote the Middle English poem *Sir Gawain and the Green Knight*. The single manuscript, now in the British Library, contains the earliest known rendering of the now famous tale. Although the author was a contemporary of Chaucer, he has never been satisfactorily identified and it is unclear as to exactly how well known the story was among his contemporaries. The story itself is a simple one, and one that is built upon far older foundations. It begins with Arthur and his court celebrating New Year's Day with feasting and tales of daring deeds. Then, as the feast reaches its height, a giant green figure riding a green horse and carrying a magnificent axe makes an appearance. The Green Knight challenges Arthur and his knights to play a game with him. One of them may take the axe and attempt to sever the Green Knight's head in exchange for the Green Knight to have the right to return the blow in a year and a day. The winner of the competition is to keep the splendid axe as his trophy.

At first, none of the knights take up the challenge, clearly worried by the supernatural aspect of the Green Knight, and Arthur himself offers to take part in the game. However, his youngest knight, Sir Gawain, begs to be allowed to undertake the challenge. Gawain severs the Green Knight's head with a single blow. However, rather than dropping down dead, the Green Knight picks up the head, remounts his horse and reminds Gawain that he is to meet him in the Green Chapel in a year and a day's time, when the blow shall be returned. The rest of the poem recounts Gawain's adventures on his quest to fulfil his obligations, culminating in his meeting with the Green Knight who, in recognition of his chivalry, strikes him only a slight blow that leaves him with a small cut to his neck. The story is one of a whole tradition of quest cycles that promote the concepts of chivalry, loyalty and courage. Gawain emerges from the tale as a flawed hero, but a hero who, in recognising those flaws within himself, is seen as a model for the chivalric Christian warrior.

In the original manuscript, the unknown author goes into some detail concerning the fitting-out of Sir Gawain prior to his embarking upon the quest to fulfil his vow. His tunic, arms and armour are described in turn before finally he is handed his shield. Upon the 'shining scarlet' shield is painted a pentangle in 'pure gold'. The author then states that 'why the pentangle was appropriate to that prince I intend to say, though it will stall our story'. He then launches into a lengthy digression, one of the only ones in the poem, in which the author details the symbolism of the pentangle – and it does indeed stall the story. It is, he states, the symbol of Solomon that 'is taken to this day as a token of fidelity' and is known in England as the 'endless knot'. He then goes on to detail the five times five ways in which the symbol will protect and inspire the knight. It is a symbol of the five wounds that Christ suffered upon the cross, of his five faultless fingers, of the five senses, of the five joys of the Virgin Mary in her son and, lastly, of the five virtues of knighthood – the 'pure pentangle as people have called it'.

It is the purity of the symbol itself, echoing the Greek idea of geometric perfection, that gave it power within the medieval mind. To the Gawain author, it was 'a five-pointed form which never failed, never stronger to one side or slack at the other, but unbroken in its being from beginning to end'. This pure, unfailing and unbroken symbol also had one other particular and widely recognised power – to offer protection from demons. As the Gawain author highlights, the pentangle was regarded as the symbol of Solomon. According to Jewish, Christian and Islamic tradition, the symbol of Solomon was found inscribed in a ring that was delivered to the great king by angels. The ring gave its bearer many powers, including the ability to talk to animals, and very specifically gave Solomon power over demons. Solomon used the ring as a signet, signing documents and decrees, and the symbol, with numerous variations, became known as the 'Seal of Solomon'. Although more usually regarded as being the six-pointed star, known today as the Star of David, many early traditions have the pentangle and Star of David as being interchangeable, as is clearly the case with the Gawain author.

The pentangle on the shield of Sir Gawain can, therefore, be viewed in a number of different lights. Although it represents all the overtly Christian religious and knightly virtues that the unknown author ascribed to it, it would also have been seen by most of the original fourteenth-century readers of the poem as a potent protection from demons. Its location upon both Gawain's shield and mantle is particularly significant. The physical protection of the knight's shield was being augmented, perhaps even enhanced, by the addition of the pentangle. Though the shield itself offered protection from the dangers of the physical world, the symbol emblazed upon it in 'pure gold' offered protection from the dangers of the spiritual or supernatural worlds. The power of this symbol in the medieval mind is clear. Gawain, the most Christian knight, carries an image of the Virgin Mary upon the inside of his shield, 'so by catching her eye his courage would not crack'. However, upon the outside of his shield, the side that would face his foes and the dangers of battle, he carries not the image of Christ or the cross but the protection of the pentangle. This concept of the pentangle being regarded as a powerful symbol of protection, particularly with regard to demons, appears clear in several examples of medieval-church graffiti. But while the protective function of the symbol appears straightforward, the uses to which it is put in a number of graffiti examples suggest that the form of protection could be subtly altered to fit specific circumstances.

The east side of the chancel arch at St Mary's church in Troston, Suffolk, is covered in a large amount of graffiti inscriptions. The lower areas of the stonework have been so covered with inscriptions as to make many of them now impossible to decipher amid the jumble of symbols and lettering. The text that can be read, and many of the symbols and images, clearly suggest that most of the graffiti dates to the late Middle Ages. Full-length figures with hands raised in prayer sit alongside symbols of the ragged staff, medieval shoe outlines, Latin inscriptions, crosses and numerous personal names. On the south side of the arch, in an area just above the crowded and jumbled mass of graffiti, sits a single and distinct inscription of a demon's head. The head is shown in profile, with its mouth gaping open like the hell mouths of medieval wall paintings and manuscript illustration, showing a row of sharp pointed teeth. A long tongue lolls out of the mouth and the whole gives the effect of the demon grinning evilly, as though about to bite down upon some Christian soul. The imagery of the demon's head is very similar to that shown on the Wenhaston Doom in Suffolk and a painted graffito from the rood stair turret at St Edmund's church, Acle, in Norfolk, and it is tempting to suggest that the Troston demon may well have been modelled upon a once-visible demon painted on the other face of the arch as part of the now very fragmented Doom.

Across the surface of the Troston demon, etched far more deeply into the stonework than the demon's head itself, is a large pentangle. The pentangle sits precisely on top of the head, with each of its points reaching the edge of the image but proceeding no further. Although not obscuring the image, the pentangle is very clearly related to the shape of the head itself. The depth of the inscription points to it having been overscored time and time again, suggesting that it was important that the symbol be clearly visible. At the other end of the church, inscribed into the tower arch, is one of the few graffiti inscriptions from the late Middle Ages that clearly depicts a woman. The full-length figure shows a woman in profile with a long, low-waisted gown and elaborate head-dress and hands raised in prayer. Clearly depicted in an act of devotion, the figure is accompanied by another deeply cut example of a pentangle. However, unlike the example from the chancel arch, this pentangle is not crossing the figure itself and sits just to one side of the image. This pattern, of pentangles crossing demonic figures, but lying alongside more human figures, is repeated in several other churches. The church of St Mary at Horne in Surrey has an example of a small demonic head complete with horns that is overlaid with a deeply etched six-pointed star. At Swannington church in Norfolk, a number of stylised human heads are etched into the pillars of the north arcade, with pentangles lying alongside them.

If we accept that the five- and six-pointed star, or Seal of Solomon, were regarded as symbols of protection during the later Middle Ages, as detailed in *Sir Gawain and the Green Knight*, with particular power to protect from the malign influence of demons, then it is possible to hazard an explanation for the recorded graffiti inscriptions. It appears clear that, where a graffito depicts a demon itself, as at Horne or Troston, the star is placed directly on top of the image. This ritual placement can be interpreted as overlaying the sign of protection across the threat, thereby neutralising that same threat. The demon has been placed beneath the seal, pinned to the wall, and its power is broken. The demon is literally pinned to the stonework beneath a never-ending line from which it cannot escape. The depth of the incised lines of the pentangle at Troston also suggests a repeated scoring of the mark, perhaps ensuring the continued imprisonment of the malign force or reinforcing the protection from evil. The same protective power of the pentangle is also to be seen in the images of people, friends and family that the symbols are found lying alongside. In these cases, that same symbol was being used not to entrap the forces of evil but, rather, to drive it away; to keep safe those whom it was inscribed next to. Put simply, the pentangle over the top of an image of a demon was a way of asking for protection *from* such evil, while that shown next to a human was asking for protection *for* that individual. Perhaps most interesting of all is that these same methods of using the pentangle as a symbol of protection are to be found all over the country, suggesting that this belief, though not appearing within the orthodox teachings of the church, was both widespread and commonly understood – a universally accepted defence against the forces of darkness.

All this talk of demons and pentangles in the context of a church may seem a little unusual when regarded from a purely modern perspective. We view churches as places of saints, angels and prayers, rather than devils and demons. However, the medieval church was a very, very different one from the church we know today. It may have been full of saints' images, but it was also a church that liked to advertise and make plain the consequences of sin and rebellion against the word of God and scripture. While the fires and the torments of hell could be conjured up by the words of the parish priest, and images of those torments placed upon the wall, such as in the thirteenth-century wall painting at Chaldon in Surrey, the embodiment of the evil that awaited the cowed churchgoers lay with the physical forms of the demons. These demons, they knew deep within their souls, lay all around them, waiting for them to fall away from the ways of the church and into their clutches. It was these demons who were responsible for the failure of crops, the sudden death of friends and the illness of children. They were as much a reality as the plagues that tore their communities apart and, as such, needed to be defended against. Here, on the walls of the church, was the battleground between good and evil, salvation and damnation, and the images of demons and pentangles were the front line in a battle for their very souls.

CHAPTER SEVEN

SWASTIKAS AND THE VIRGIN: WITCH MARKS

'Solomon's Knot' or 'Swastika Pelta' design, Litcham, Norfolk

'So none can study and put into practice . . . the circles and art of magic, without committing an horrible defection from God'

King James I/VI, Daemonologie, 1597

Many of the seemingly apotropaic symbols recorded among collections of church graffiti have an obscure relationship to the orthodox beliefs of the medieval church. But there are others that appear to stem from a recognisable and traceable source. One of the most common symbols discovered in medieval churches, and in post-medieval domestic buildings, is the 'VV' symbol. Often shown inverted to resemble a capital 'M', or even upon its side, this particular symbol has been recorded on stonework, tombs, woodwork and plaster. It can be found carved into the rood screens, the lead of the font, on the back of the main door and, at sites like Castle Acre in Norfolk, can even be seen lurking beneath numerous layers of Reformation limewash. Purely in terms of quantity, its appearance apparently outweighs the entire collection of other ritual protection marks by a ratio of nearly two to one. However, despite this frequency, it has been difficult to identify any particular or recognisable distribution patterns.

The symbol has been traditionally associated with the cult of the Virgin Mary – the 'VV' suggested as being the initial letters of the term 'Virgo Virginum' (Virgin of Virgins). When shown the other way up, as an 'M', it is thought to represent the name 'Maria', again a reference to the Virgin Mary. Although this may very well be the case with the obviously medieval examples, the fact is that the symbol clearly continues to be used well into the eighteenth century – with occasional examples turning up even in nineteenth-century contexts – making it likely that, although a 'traditional' marking, its meaning may well have changed or evolved over time. Indeed, it would most certainly be difficult to argue that an individual creating such a symbol in a farmhouse in the late eighteenth century in an environment entirely divorced from the belief system of the medieval church by several centuries, was creating it with the same intended function as an individual inscribing it into a church pillar in the fifteenth century. It appears, instead, that its meaning altered slightly, moving away from obvious religious associations until, like many other traditions that quietly pass down the ages, it was seen simply as something that was there to bring 'good luck' and might, perhaps, keep ill fortune at bay.

Given the supposed association with medieval examples and the Virgin Mary, it has been suggested that the symbol is more likely to be recorded in areas of the church associated with Marian imagery, such as the Lady Chapel or the Mary altar. Although several churches have shown such a distribution pattern, they are most certainly in the minority. In general terms, and based upon the surveys carried out in many hundreds of churches, the symbol would appear to be fairly indiscriminate in terms of its location. It is, indeed, as likely to be recorded on the back of rood screens, around doorways and on pews as it is to be found near any area that might have, or once have had, Marian associations. At Ashwell church, already highlighted for the number of ritual protection marks it contains, a mass concentration of these 'VV' symbols can be seen on the wall near the north side of the tower arch, an area that has no obvious connection with the Virgin Mary or any particular saint.

The 'VV' symbol is also one of the few ritual protection marks that made the occasional crossover into more orthodox church art. The west door of Fakenham church in north Norfolk contains a highly decorative 'flint flushwork' shield in each of the spandrels. One is a monogram of the name 'MARIA', being a reference to the Virgin Mary, while the other contains the enigmatic 'VV' symbol. The symbol is also to be found decorating cast-iron firebacks, as a motif on decorative floor tiles and on memorial brasses of individuals set into the floor of parish churches. Not only did this symbol manage to cross the great divide between the graffiti and orthodox decoration, it also managed to cross the chasm of the English Reformation, a feat that most other symbols found among church graffiti do not manage.

One of the other best-known symbols that has apotropaic associations is the 'swastika pelta', or Solomon's knot motif. The name swastika pelta is one that, despite many people's best attempts to the latter, appears to have stuck, although it is wrong on just about every level. The term was first coined, we think, by the legendary and fantastically moustached archaeologist Sir Mortimer Wheeler to describe a design that he kept coming across on the Roman mosaics that he was studying.

Early-graffiti scholar Violet Pritchard then continued with the swastika-pelta term in her 1967 book *English Medieval Graffiti*, even arguing that it was the more correct term than Solomon's knot as Solomon had supposedly lived in the Iron Age. It now appears that we are unshakably stuck with it. Pritchard spent a good deal of energy examining the examples that she came across in her study of the churches around Cambridge, and even dedicated an entire appendix in her book to the subject. She came to a number of interesting conclusions concerning its use and distribution. However, it is an indication of just how far the study of church graffiti has come in the last few years that we can now examine the subject again and, respectfully, put aside many of Pritchard's conclusions.

It is actually worth noting that what Pritchard did with regard to this particular design was really quite remarkable. She came to the conclusion that this was a design found 'in many churches' that contained early graffiti, but she really could not have been further from the truth. The recent large-scale surveys have shown that the symbol is actually exceedingly rare, with less than three dozen examples found so far throughout the whole of England. How, then, did Pritchard manage to come to the opposite conclusion? The answer is a simple one: she was most uncommonly lucky. It appears that in her limited travels, Pritchard just happened to wander into the two dozen or so churches in East Anglia that contain this symbol, a feat of serendipity that many archaeologists would give their right arm for. With surveys having now been carried out in almost half the churches in East Anglia, which was Pritchard's main search area, only a bare handful of other examples have ever come to light.

However, one of the conclusions reached by Pritchard is less easy to put aside. In her appendix to *English Medieval Graffiti*, she suggested that the vast majority of the swastika-pelta designs were to be found at churches that were either built upon or near ancient religious sites or were located on the route of Roman roads; again, suggesting an ancient origin. Even taking into account the new discoveries, the idea is difficult to disprove. This might simply be because many medieval churches *were* built on religious ancient sites, with the early Christians tending to favour just such sites to ensure that their new religion did not seem entirely alien to the local population. After all, the Anglo-Saxon kingdoms had been building churches for centuries prior to the church-building frenzy that occurred in the early Norman period, and these Anglo-Saxon churches did, it appears, tend to favour earlier religious sites. In addition, it must also be noted that the Romans did build rather an extensive road system throughout East Anglia, and few villages and churches are ever more than a short walk away from the route of at least a minor Roman highway. However, until further evidence comes to light, it is certainly a theory that is worth further thought.

Like the compass-drawn daisy wheel or hexfoil, the swastika pelta appears on a large number of early Norman church decorations, most notably the fonts and above the doorways on the tympanum. It has an ancient pedigree, stretching back well beyond the Roman period, and it appears to share many of the same apotropaic functions as the hexfoil as well, being a variety of endless-knot design that was thought to confuse and entrap evil spirits. At certain churches, such as in Lidgate, the design also appears to copy the distribution pattern of the hexfoil designs, being concentrated in the area around which the font used to sit. However, it is also to be found in some very unusual places. At Litcham in Norfolk, a single example can be found halfway along the north arcade, but appears to be entirely alone and not associated with any other graffiti. Similarly, an unfinished example in Norwich Cathedral is actually tucked away in a niche to one side of the choir, and only a few metres away from the bishop's throne, a position that suggests it can only have been created by a member of the cathedral community.

Beyond these symbols there are a mass of other markings that have been, at one time or another, considered to be ritual protection marks. A ladder motif, found at a number of churches, such as Fincham in Norfolk and Parham in Suffolk, has also been described as a witch mark. Linked to the story of Jacob's ladder, these motifs are generally thought of as being associated with the idea of salvation and the climb away from evil. However, they are a rare find and it is difficult to decide whether any such link may have existed in the minds of those people who actually made them. A zigzag motif that looks more like a haphazard scratch on the stonework has been interpreted as a lightning strike and, therefore, a symbol used to ward off the very real threat of storms. In a time before the establishment of any formal fire service, lightning could all too easily begin a fire that could quickly destroy a whole settlement, and the number of great fires recorded in English towns in the sixteenth and seventeenth centuries certainly highlights the fact that such tragedies were all too common. Many folk beliefs were concerned with the possibility of lightning strikes, and the survival of many of these beliefs until very recent years does rather suggest that the fear was a very real one. Oak timbers, particularly those made from a tree that had been struck by lightning, were believed to be immune from being struck again (lightning rarely striking the same place twice) and were therefore sought after when building a house. Indeed, the central panels of rood screens also appear to have been made from oak and it may be for this reason that many of these little lightning strikes are found scratched into the rear of these screens. The association between lightning and oak also appears to have been transferred across to the symbol of the acorn, although few images of acorns are found among the graffiti. This folk belief appears to have been carried on into homes even after the invention of electricity. Equating electricity with lightning, people attached acorns to the cords of light switches; a phenomenon whose echoes can still be seen in the turned wooden acorns that hang from light-pull cords even today. It appears that while our houses and utilities may have entered the modern world, our hearts and souls still link us back to a darker past – whether we are aware of it or not.

CHAPTER EIGHT

CROSSES OF FAITH

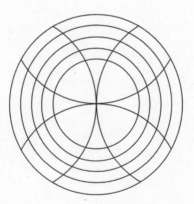

Typical compass-drawn 'Consecration Cross' design

'When once thy foot enters the church, be bare.
God is more there, then thou: for thou art there
Onely by his permission. Then beware,
And make thy self all reverence and fear.
Kneeling ne're spoil'd silk stocking: quit thy state.
All equall are within the churches gate.'

'The Church Porch', George Herbert (1593–1633)

If I were to state that one of the most common pieces of early graffiti to be recorded in medieval churches were inscriptions in the form of the cross, no one would be terribly surprised. That a Christian building is covered in Christian symbolism isn't exactly earth-shattering news. Nobody is going to hold the front page. However, as with most things relating to early graffiti, the crosses etched into the stones of hundreds of English churches cannot be explained in as straightforward a manner as you might at first suspect. First, these crosses aren't exactly where you would expect them to be. Although you will come across the occasional cross within the main body of the church, as at North Elmham in Norfolk or West Wittering in West Sussex, the vast majority of all the graffiti crosses that have been recorded are invariably around the doorways or in the church porch. There does seem to be a bias towards the south door, which was the most usual entrance to the church, but it isn't too unusual to find them etched into the jambs of the north door, too. If a porch is present, then the graffiti can often be found scattered around the area, although, again, a concentration around the door is still likely. In some churches the number of these crosses is really quite remarkable, with sites such as Ludham and Colkirk, both in Norfolk, each having as many as a dozen of these crosses. These crosses are also clearly not just an East Anglian phenomenon, with churches such as Stodmarsh in Kent, Stoke Orchard in Gloucestershire, Godalming in Surrey and Wootton Wawen in Warwickshire all being notable for the sheer number of crosses still visible around their doorways. The style of the crosses can also vary tremendously. Some are no more than lightly scratched 'X' markings that are almost impossible to see without specialist lighting. Others, such as the rather beautiful example from Ludham, can be deeply etched and very neatly drawn, making it visible to just about anyone passing through the doorway even today.

The fact that many of these crosses are so deeply cut into the stonework has meant that they have been known about and recorded for rather a long time. As far back as the late eighteenth and early nine-teenth centuries, local vicars and rectors, who invariably doubled up as the local historian and antiquarian, noted these crosses and pondered their meaning. The answer they came up with, perhaps unsurprisingly, was that these were pilgrim crosses, small symbols scratched into the door surrounds by those undertaking the popular pastime of pilgrimage during the Middle Ages. What these antiquarians couldn't decide upon, though, was exactly why these crosses had been carved. Blaming the devout, and a few undoubtedly less-than-devout, pilgrims was a neat answer – but it was still only half an answer. Were these carved by those ready to take a vow of pilgrimage? Did these crosses represent the vow itself, carved there as an act of faith and undertaking? Or were these carved by pilgrims who had returned safely to the parish from which they had set out, wanting to leave a mark of thanksgiving for their safe return? Even today, church guidebooks and local church-wardens will each put their own particular spin upon the tale, with the story changing from place to place and church to church, and sometimes from day to day.

The problem with this satisfyingly neat interpretation is that the ancient vicars and antiquarians really didn't have any evidence to back up their theory that these crosses were created by pilgrims. They had simply found a story that explained the existence of the graffiti, put it forward as one possible interpretation, and, with no other obvious or documented answer coming forth, it has become regarded as fact as the decades and centuries have passed. In reality, the theory has nothing to support it except continued usage. Having said that, it would be wrong to suggest that the idea was plucked out of the air, or that it was the whim of those looking for a deeply religious explanation. Many of these early antiquarians did indeed have experience of medieval pilgrim sites, and it is likely that some of them had travelled to the Holy Land and the most holy of medieval sites: the Church of the Holy Sepulchre in Jerusalem. Here they would have come across several areas of the building that were quite literally covered in small carved crosses. These, they would have been told by their local guides, had been carved by the devout pilgrims as a symbol of their objective achieved. It would, therefore, have been an all-too-simple and logical step for the antiquar-ians to have concluded that the small crosses carved into the door surrounds of their own parish churches in England were also the work of pilgrims at the other end of their arduous journey.

As logical as such an explanation may at first seem, the lack of evidence is a problem. The only early written reference to someone actually making one of these crosses is, at the very least, ambiguous. An early-twelfth-century biography of the female mystic Christina of Markyate recounts that, as a child, she was discovered scratching a 'devotional cross' on the door of St Alban's Abbey. These little crosses are so numerous and so widespread that they clearly had a meaning and an intended function – but exactly what this 'devotional' meaning was remains unclear. If they were made by departing or arriving pilgrims, then why are they almost always located around the doorways or in the porch? Surely, if they were acts of devotion, they would have been more effective if placed in a more spiritually significant part of the building, such as near an altar or chapel, rather than out in the porch? We know that the insides of churches were covered in graffiti inscriptions, many of which were clearly devotional, so why then could the 'pilgrim' crosses not be created there as well? It would appear far more likely that the meaning of these crosses is in fact related to their location, and that they are most probably linked to something, or some activity, that was taking place at the church door or within the porch.

The church entrance and porch generally have very little significance in the modern church. In most churches, the porch tends to be the place where you will find the parish noticeboard, the water bowl for visiting dogs and the faded and wilting remains of last week's flower display. It is very much a place that people briefly pass through to get from outside to inside, or perhaps take shelter from the English summer weather. However, that wasn't the case during the Middle Ages. Back then, the porch was regarded as a much more significant area of the church, with a religious and social function that went far beyond being something to purely keep the rain away from the door. In religious terms, a number of the church services, such as the marriage ceremony, the churching of women after childbirth and the burial service, actually took place in the porch or at the church door. The best known of these is perhaps the wedding ceremony, which, for many centuries, largely took place with the parish priest facing the intended couple at the church door. Medieval and Tudor documents make it clear that only those of high social status were allowed to be married within the main body of the church, and even then there were distinctions for rank. The son or daughter of an earl, for example, could be married near the altar at the entrance to the choir, while a more humble knight could only expect to be married within the main door of the church. For those of lower station – which meant in reality just about everyone – then the ceremony was to take place outside the main door and, if there was one, inside the church porch. The priest would take up station at the door, physically barring the couple from entering the building and, only after the vows had been made, and rings or tokens exchanged, would he move aside and lead the couple into the church for the first time as man and wife, where a Mass would then be celebrated. In England, this custom continued well into the sixteenth century, and it isn't until the publication of the Book of Common Prayer in 1549 that we see that 'the persons to be married shal come into the body of the Churche, wyth theyr friends and neighbours'.

The religious functions of the church porch and entrance didn't merely revolve around the services that took place there. The porch itself, from at least as far back as the ninth century, was seen as one of the most honoured places of burial for the departed. The early church frowned upon burial within the main body of the building, and passed numerous edicts outlawing the practice. Indeed, in the very early days of the Christian church – and probably reflecting the Roman practice of burial outside the town or city walls – the church even discouraged bodies being interred in the churchyard. Over the centuries, local habit and tradition began to erode church legislation and churchyard burials became increasingly common. However, even the ninth-century Council of Metz, which recognised that it was fighting a losing battle against burial in the porch and churchyard, stated that only those of the very highest rank, such as abbots or bishops, were to be accorded burial within the church itself. Therefore, the closest that even the most respected citizen could get to burial within the church for much of the early Middle Ages was to be buried within the porch.

The porch is also often home to a holy-water stoup, a small basin-like container in which holy water was placed. Upon entering and leaving the church, the parishioners were expected to dip their fingers in the water and make the sign of the cross upon their forehead or breast.

Although this action is traditionally thought of as being a renewal of the vows of baptism, it is recorded that it was also seen as an effective method of warding off evil. The early seventeenth-century mystic, St Teresa of Avila, stated that 'there is nothing that puts the Devils to flight like holy water'. The church's use of holy water as a protective and curative is well documented. As late as the middle of the sixteenth century, the inhabitants of Canterbury called upon the church to give them holy water to sprinkle upon their homes during a particularly violent storm, believing that it would protect them from the lightning and drive out any evil spirits. The use of holy water against evil, and its well-recorded use in many medieval charms and enchantments, made it a precious and sought-after commodity by those involved in folk magic and healing – much to the concern of church authorities. As far back as 1236, Archbishop Edmund Rich recommended that church fonts should be fitted with lids that could be locked, for fear that the holy water would be stolen and used in acts of 'witchcraft'. How this restriction of access to holy water affected the holy water stoup in the porch is unclear, and it must be assumed that, unlike today, it was only filled with water just prior to service times.

The church porch was not reserved solely for religious activities, and the evidence points towards it acting as the administrative centre for the medieval parish. It was here that people came to draw up agreements, sign contracts and witness documents, and a number of surviving medieval manuscripts describe this. The porch acted as the de-facto parish office and, in many of the elaborate late-medieval two-storey church porches, the upper room was indeed often noted as being both vestry and parish office. In some cases, the upper room in the porch also acted as the parish armoury, where arms and armour were stored for use by the local militia in times of conflict. In medieval Scandinavia, the word for porch actually translates as 'weapon-store', although it is unclear whether this is because weapons were actually stored here, or whether this is where they had to be left by individuals before entering the church building. In the upper room of the church porch at Mendlesham in Suffolk, you can still see the Tudor arms and armour that have been stored there since before the time of the Armada, still hanging upon the original wooden pegs, awaiting an invasion that never came – a truly unique survival in England.

The church porch was also noted as the place that people came to swear affidavits and formalise verbal agreements and, in common with today's continued practice, actually was the place where legal documents and notices were displayed. It was at the church door that the whole Protestant movement can be said to have begun, with the reformer Martin Luther supposedly nailing his ninety-five theses to the door of All Saints' church in Wittenberg. This idea, that people came to make agreements at the church door and in the church porch, is of particular interest, as many of these documents are signed using crosses. This has usually been seen as a sign that the people involved were illiterate, not even being able to write their own names, but this is no longer thought to always be the case. There have been a number of instances where individuals have signed certain documents with a cross and others with their own names, suggesting it was actually a conscious decision on their part as to which one they decided to use. Perhaps then, in these cases, the use of the cross was meant to represent far more than just somebody 'making their mark'? Perhaps the cross was a positive action that either suggested divine approval of, or asked for a blessing upon, the agreement? This could also be the case with verbal agreements made at the church door. The inscribed cross would not only act as a visual and permanent reminder to all parties of the agreement, but it would also ask for the church's blessing upon it.

The one thing that many of these church-porch activities had in common, be it the marriage service or the swearing of affidavits, is that many of them involved the taking or making of vows. In the Middle Ages, vows, oaths and pledges, particularly those made in the sight of God, were seen as only being breakable with the most severe of consequences. While the breaking of such a vow might lead to local disputes, angry neighbours, lasting hostility and bad feeling on earth, the spiritual consequences would have been far higher. The Bible made it clear that oaths were sacred undertakings, and an oath-breaker was committing a grievous sin that he would be called to account for on the Day of Judgement – and for eternity. Perhaps, then, each of these crosses represents a physical symbol of these oaths and vows made before the church door? Perhaps each one represents a solemn and spiritual contract, a deal between an individual's soul and the Almighty, each cross around the church door a vow not lightly undertaken. Whether these vows were relating to local agreements, to the bonds of marriage or to a journey promised will probably never be known for certain – but it is just possible, perhaps, that some may indeed have been made by pilgrims.

CHAPTER NINE

MAGIC ON THE WALLS: CHARMS AND CURSES

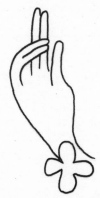

A hand raised in blessing, Worlington, Suffolk

'It is said, if thou wilt make a ring of a fresh myrtle tree, and put it on thy ring finger, it mitigateth or extincteth the impostume under the arm holes'

The Book of Secrets of Albertus Magnus, *C16th*

While many of the markings and graffiti found in English medieval churches fall into the categories of ritual protection marks, devotional graffiti or prayers, there are many others that were obviously meant to have a specific spiritual 'function' that fell well outside what we might consider the normal boundary of the orthodox church. These inscriptions might share similarities with some of the devotional graffiti and prayers, but it is clear that they go beyond what we would today consider acceptable practice. These inscriptions, to our modern eyes at least, appear to be related to areas that some scholars term 'lay piety', one aspect of which – to put it simply – is 'magic'.

The definition of medieval magic is actually far from simple. The regular and unquestionable transformation of the wine and bread during the Mass into the blood and body of Christ – or transubstantiation, as it is known – was not regarded as magical. However, the recovery of stolen goods using a book and a key, or the searching-out of buried treasure with the help of demon guides, most probably was. The fact that both of the latter activities were recorded as having been carried out by both priests and monks rather suggests that the dividing line between the acceptable and unacceptable magic of the church, if it existed at all, was rather a hazy one. As we have seen, the ritual protection marks that cover English churches appear to have been an accepted and acceptable part of the experience of religion at a parish level. They may not have been officially sanctioned by the church, or turn up in official church documents, but they were most certainly known about, understood and used by a large proportion of the medieval population. To go beyond the use of these markings, and to begin to dabble in the making of charms or magical amulets, was to invite serious interest from the church authorities. Many a 'wise woman' or 'cunning man', as the white witches of medieval England were known, found themselves being investigated by the church at some point in their lives. However, no matter what charms they had created, or what cures they had supposedly effected, the vast majority of them could argue that no magic was involved, and that all they did was direct and invoke the help of God. Such was the ambiguous nature of the boundary between prayer, miracles and magic that, in many cases, even the church authorities found it difficult to judge whether any offence had actually taken place.

The everyday activities of many of these white witches is fairly well documented – in many cases from notes taken at depositions against them – and it is fair to say that much of what they dealt with would today fall into the catch-all category of folk magic. While they would certainly involve themselves in the creation of charms to counteract the evil eye, or help in the recovery of stolen goods, much of their time appears to have been taken up dealing with medical complaints and ailments. In a world before scientific medical treatment, their cures, aids and remedies formed the backbone of the parish medical services, treating everything from warts to birth complications, migraines to terminal illness. One of the most common ways for these cunning folk to proceed would be to prescribe a cure, in whatever form, that would often be accompanied by some form of written charm. In cases where the charm was written upon parchment, it was often stated as part of the cure that the piece of parchment was to be carried or worn by the patient until the full cure had been effected. It is these type of charms, most specifically those concerned with healing and ailments, that are to be found repeated in the graffiti inscriptions of our churches.

We are lucky in the fact that we actually have quite a large number of medieval and Tudor charms written on parchment that survive to the present day. Often found hidden inside old buildings, or bundled up with other manuscript collections, these written charms are wonderful first-hand evidence of the type of magic employed throughout England. Today, these charms are cared for in our museums and record offices and they have been the subject of considerable serious study. Some are more general charms, against such things as an 'evil death', while others offer a general protection from evil for both humans and their livestock; but there are also many charms that were believed to be particularly powerful when used against certain ailments or events. Ritual charms to protect against lightning can be found alongside charms against the fistula and charms to help a woman conceive a child.

The late-fifteenth-century commonplace book of Robert Reynes of Acle in Norfolk contains an interesting selection of just such charms. Reynes was born somewhere about 1450, and, like his father before him, became churchreeve (churchwarden) at the church of St Edmund. The family appear to have been reasonably comfortable but seem never to have entered the upper ranks of local society. Reynes, as can be expected of someone holding even local rank within the church, was fairly meticulous in his record keeping, and this is reflected in his commonplace book. Such books are rare survivals from the period. Part almanac, part diary and part notebook, a commonplace book was where Reynes made note of any items that he felt were of significance, or items that he wanted to refer back to at a later date. His own book contains a diverse selection of material. Alongside an important copy of the 'Life of St Anne' can be found fragments of a morality play, charts of weights and measures, orders copied down for the local constables of the watch, notes on astrology, the rules of bloodletting and notes concerning land transactions and family history. Reynes also appears to have made use of the book as a sort of spiritual primer, and included poems concerning the seven deadly sins, the seven sacraments and various 'improving' phrases and sayings. Interspersed with these texts is a fascinating collection of contemporary charms, obviously included by Reynes so he could refer to them later. These include charms for the cure of fever, the falling sickness (epilepsy), a charm calling upon St Apollonia for the cure of toothache, charms against general dangers, sickness and an elaborate ritualised charm, involving setting a small child in the sun, for making angels appear. The book sadly does not go into any detail about what was to happen when the angels actually made an appearance.

The charms that appear in Robert Reynes's commonplace book, and in numerous others of the preserved manuscripts, are also to be found on the walls of our churches. Charms against the fistula are to be found at Worlington in Suffolk, Carlisle Cathedral and Colkirk, Norfolk; while at Lidgate in Suffolk, there is a charm of unknown usage that is almost exactly identical to one found in a manuscript now in the British Library. Numerous examples of inscriptions showing patterns of concentric circles, within which are located crosses or pentangles, appear in churches across the country, and are also to be found in a late-fifteenth-century 'leech book' (a book containing medical recipes) as a charm against the plague. At Bardney in Lincolnshire, there is a floriated cross within a circle, described in a contemporary manuscript as a 'magic circle', perhaps associated with the five wounds of Christ. The number of possible magic circles found among the graffiti inscriptions is potentially huge. However, there is also a large problem with their interpretation. There are so very many circles found among church graffiti that in many cases it is difficult to decide whether the circles are meant to be part of an architectural inscription, a ritual protection mark, an astrological chart or part of a charm. In particular, the number of circular inscriptions that could have been created as part of an astrological chart makes interpretation sometimes all but impossible.

As shown in Robert Reynes's commonplace book, it is impossible to consider the medieval belief in these charms without taking into account their creators' fundamental faith in astrology. Although today considered, at best, a pseudo-science, astrology was an integral part of everyday life and belief during the Middle Ages. The belief was that the wisdom that could be found among the study of the stars and planets was not just limited to the idea of foretelling the future, but was a part of medieval life. The medical men of the period believed that the body and health were governed by the four 'humours', which in turn were influenced by the stars, so astrology was, understandably, regarded as just one facet of all medicine. Therefore, if you approached someone on the matters of health, whether a physician, witch or cunning man, the first thing that they would do would be to cast your personal horoscope. Likewise, it was a brave individual who began a new undertaking or started a long journey without first having their horoscope cast. Although exact figures for the Middle Ages are hard to come by, the surviving casebooks for the seventeenth-century astrologer William Lilly reveal that at the peak of his popularity he was consulted nearly two thousand times a year. Such was the level of belief in astrology that, until the later Tudor period, it was actually considered an act of treason to cast the horoscope of the monarch.

Many medieval astrological charts and horoscopes appear to have taken the form of concentric circles, and a large number of these survive in manuscript form and, later, in printed works on the subject. The circles – or celestial spheres as they were known – were the orbs to which the fixed stars and planets were attached, and the methods by which they rotated around the earth. This basic model remained fixed until the beginning of the sixteenth century, when Nicolaus Copernicus put forward the idea that the planets revolved around the sun rather than around the earth. However, despite making a major advance in respect of the structure of the solar system, even Copernicus still believed in the concept of the celestial sphere. Any astrological predictions and interpretations had to plot and take into account the position of these celestial spheres at the time of casting the horoscope. This was done with the use of complex planetary and star charts, which could be used to create an individual chart that represented a particular point in time; and these often appear as collections of concentric circles representing the celestial spheres. Upon this base would be overlaid the markings of individual planets and stars. Such charts of concentric circles, both with and without meaningful additional marks, can be found in hundreds of churches across the country. The problem, of course, is deciding exactly which marks are actually meaningful. With many of the surfaces upon which they were created being badly eroded and worn, the difference between a mark meant to denote the position of a plant and a mark caused by a clumsy workman or churchwarden are all but indistinguishable.

Assuming that all these markings are not just the work of badly coordinated workmen then we must ask ourselves exactly why they chose to inscribe them into the walls of the church? If such charms were deemed to work when written out on parchment, then what was the advantage, if any, of etching them into the stonework? The answer, I believe, must be the same reason that was given for the ritual protection marks: that by inscribing them into the church building, which was seen as spiritually powerful and significant, they were in some way enhancing the power of these charms. They were, in effect, calling upon God and the saints to validate these charms and help ensure a successful conclusion and, like Robert Reynes and his commonplace book, felt no compulsion to separate their own charms from the prayers of the orthodox church.

With the walls of our medieval churches covered in many, many examples of folk magic and strange beliefs, it really should not seem strange to us to also find evidence that those very same walls were once also covered in 'curses' – and yet it does. The idea makes many people uncomfortable. Most probably, this is simply the association people have between 'curses' and black magic and, more particularly, witchcraft. Witches and their curses have filled centuries' worth of our literature, folk tales and fairy stories; everything from Macbeth's three witches on the blasted heath to the evil witch who can send an entire castle full of people to sleep for a hundred years. Curses are seen as being from the unacceptable side of faith and belief and should really have no place in a house dedicated to God and prayer. It is a distinction that carries on to the present day, with the magic presented in modern stories such as the Harry Potter books falling into the two very distinct areas of 'spells', which are thoroughly acceptable, and 'curses', which are seen largely as the domain of only evil practitioners. As a result, the finding of apparent curses among the medieval-graffiti inscriptions in our churches leaves a bad taste in many people's mouths. Indeed, the fact that such finds often lead to them being ascribed to modern Wiccans, devil worshippers or hoaxers is a sign of just how mentally remote we are today from the commonplace beliefs of the medieval church.

The medieval church was not just an institution that believed in the efficacy of curses – but one that actually made use of, and approved, its own curses. While the church may have had the standard weapons and threats of the church courts and, in extremis, excommunication in its arsenal, it was obviously felt that there were times when a more direct approach might be needed. For certain crimes – most particularly those that were aimed at the church itself or its property – the church was more than willing to offer up curses upon the guilty party. It is commonplace to find medieval manuscripts, once among the most precious of all church belongings, actually inscribed with individual 'book curses' against those who would steal or deface the work. The church also entered curses into the formal litany of everyday service, most particularly with the reading out of Chapter 28 of the Book of Deuteronomy. The chapter specifically deals with blessings and curses, including such delights as, 'Cursed shall be the fruit of thy body, and the fruit of thy land, the increase of thy kine, and the flocks of thy sheep.' In 1549, with the introduction of the Book of Common Prayer, the reading of Deuteronomy was replaced with a specific service, known as the Commination, that was to be read upon the first day of Lent and 'at other times'. The service of Commination was essentially a summary of all the curses contained in the Bible, not just within Deuteronomy, that were to be laid against those who did not respect God's commandments. The curses ranged against all sinners, from those who had 'moved his neighbour's boundary stone', to the 'fornicators, adulterers, covetous persons, idolaters, slanderers, drunkards and extortioners'. Indeed, it left little room for doubt. If you sinned against the church in word or deed, you were, quite simply, cursed.

The church could also, upon a very few significant occasions, actually fall back upon using the General Great Curse. The ceremony was usually only performed by those of the rank of bishop and above and was carried out using 'bell, book and candle'. The ceremony is thought to date back as far as the ninth century and appears to have developed out of the elaborate excommunication ceremonies of the church, when individuals would be formally denied the comfort of the sacraments and Christian worship. However, the General Great Curse took this a large step further, stating that they were to be 'accursed of God, and of his church, from the sole of their foot to the crown of their head'. One of the best recorded examples of this formal curse being actually carried out took place in Westminster Hall in 1253, when no less than thirteen fully robed bishops cursed the violators of the Magna Carta and all transgressors of the liberties of the church. At the end of the ceremony, the bells were rung, the book closed with a sound like a small thunderclap, and the candles were extinguished and cast aside – at which point the bishops cried, 'So let them be extinguished and sink into the pit of hell which run into the dangers of this sentence.'

Given the church's enthusiasm for curses, and the fact that many of the ritual protection marks and devotional graffiti appear to have been both accepted and acceptable to the everyday officers of the church, it is hardly surprising that members of the congregation didn't feel prohibited from adding their own curses to the church walls. With the dividing line between what may have been considered 'magic' and the formal devotions of the church being a distinctly hazy one – if recognised at all – it is rather unlikely that those creating these curses saw them as very different from the votive markings and prayers that they sat next to. What, after all, was a curse except a prayer for divine retribution to be called down upon those who had sinned against them? The idea was even supported by the Old Testament, which promised that God would listen to the beseeching of the unjustly wronged. Indeed, if certain signs, sigils and symbols could be relied upon to ward off the evil eye and trap demons, then could not other signs and symbols be used to attract those very same demons towards specific individuals? The logic was undeniable; it was basic common sense. And that is exactly what we are finding on the walls of our churches all over England.

Most medieval curses are usually based upon a simple concept: that a reversal, or inversion, of normal practice will invoke or invite an opposite effect. This idea isn't only limited to turning things upside down or back to front, but can also include the ritual destruction of a complete object to form a broken or imperfect one. The ideas behind such curses stretch back many thousands of years, and their origins can be found at least as far back as the Bronze Age, when precious and valued items such as bronze swords and daggers were ritually despoiled, or slighted, before being cast into deep waters or buried as offerings to the gods. And that is exactly what we are seeing among the mass of graffiti on our church walls: examples of symbols, most particularly the compass-drawn designs, that have been deliberately slighted, damaged or left unfinished. While it can easily be argued that many of these are the result of accidental damage or later vandalism, there are simply too many that share the same characteristics for it to have been entirely chance. The most compelling of the examples are the number of compass-drawn daisy wheels that have deliberately had only one single line left out. By a single line, I do not mean a complete arc of the compass, which would form the side of two of the 'petals', which could just represent an interruption that led to the motif remaining unfinished, but only half of one arc, being the side of only one 'petal'. Another factor that makes these deliberately unfinished designs less likely to be coincidental accidents is that they turn up in quite large numbers across the whole country. Examples can be seen at sites like Troston in Suffolk, Lanercost Priory in the far north of England, Winchelsea on the south coast and Lacock Abbey in Wiltshire; just about everywhere where there are good examples of early graffiti.

Far easier to recognise and interpret, although also far rarer, are the medieval written curses that adorn our church walls. In these cases, we also have quite a number of surviving curses and charms written on parchment to compare them with. Other curses have been found inscribed on stones that were then ritually buried, such as the sixteenth-century example from London that contained magical symbols and the wish that 'nothing may prosper nor go forward that Ralph Scrope taketh in hand'. However, the most common types of curse to survive in England are actually far older and date back to the Roman period. Roman curses have been discovered at a number of sites across the country and tend to be inscribed into soft material such as lead. Most of them take the same form, being a name (or names) of those to be cursed and often a detailed description of what was to happen to the individual who was cursed. It was also usual that the whole of the text, or just the name of the target, would be 'corrupted' in some manner, either inverted or with the letters jumbled up. This text was then most usually accompanied by an astrological symbol, or symbols, often that of the moon, to add to the essentially 'magical' nature of the object. The finished curse was then either ritually deposited, often in water, or nailed or attached to a spiritually significant site such as a temple or shrine.

Inscriptions almost identical in every way to these Roman curses are also to be found among the graffiti inscriptions in our medieval churches and cathedrals. Indeed, the inscriptions are so alike, despite the near thousand-year time gap, that it is difficult to think of any other way of interpreting them. In Norwich Cathedral, at least three such inscriptions have been identified, with the best-preserved example to be found towards the eastern end of the cathedral, inscribed into the stonework of the south ambulatory. The inscription is a simple example, but beautifully executed, and contains just a name and an astrological symbol. The name, cut precisely and in a well-practised script, has been entirely inverted, and reads 'Keynfford', below which is carved an unusual astrological symbol that appears to be a combination of that for the moon and the sun. The Keynford family were actually a reasonably well-known Norwich merchant family in the late Middle Ages and appear as correspondents in the Paston Letters, a fascinating account of family life, politics and intrigue in late-fifteenth-century England. Exactly what the Keynfords had done to warrant being the subject of a written curse is unknown. However, it is worth remembering that this particular curse was created by someone who was most certainly very used to writing, and was located in an area of the cathedral to which most of the population wouldn't have access to. This does rather suggest that whoever wrote the curse was actually a member of the cathedral community. Whether they created the curse due to a personal grudge against the Keynford family, or whether they created it on behalf of somebody else, it is still an intriguing insight into the workings of the medieval mind and their attitudes towards faith and belief.

CHAPTER TEN

VOYAGES OVER STONE: SHIP GRAFFITI

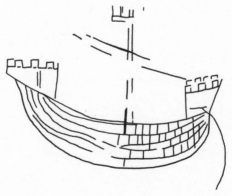

A typical early example of ship graffiti, Parham, Suffolk

'Methoughts I saw a thousand fearful wrecks,
a thousand men that fishes gnawed upon,
wedges of gold, great anchors, heaps of pearl . . .
All scattered in the bottom of the sea'

William Shakespeare, Richard III

Of all the types of early graffiti to be found in medieval churches, the one that has probably received the most attention is that known as ship graffiti. Across the walls and pillars of churches, cathedrals and chapels, images of medieval and later ships sail in a never-ending journey across the stonework. The fact that they are easily recognisable, unlike so many other types of graffiti, has probably led to the high level of interest in them. In addition, the presence of ships scratched into the walls of a medieval church immediately raises questions among the curious: Why are they there? What do they signify? Do they commemorate a hazardous sea voyage or represent a real ship; a long-since lost vessel that carried simple souls to view the wonders of far-off lands? The combination of ancient mystery and the mundane makes them a source of almost endless fascination.

Until very recently, it was believed that examples of ship graffiti were mainly confined to churches located on the coast. Seaports, in particular, such as Dover and Southampton, appeared to contain more than their fair share of examples. As a result, it became a generally held belief that these sketches were the work of the sailors themselves, or their friends and families – images of the vessels in which they hazarded their lives to make a living, or simple visual records of the objects they saw around them every day. However, as with most other types of early graffiti, more recent large-scale studies of many hundreds of churches across the country have shown that such ideas now appear to be a little too simplistic.

To begin with, it is now recognised that ship graffiti is not only to be found in the churches that line our shores. It was simply the case that many early researchers went looking for ship graffiti near the coast and – unsurprisingly – found it. More widespread searches have shown that it is not solely confined to the coastal regions, or even their immediate hinterlands. In fact, while it must be conceded that ship graffiti does tend to show a marked concentration in coastal areas, it is actually to be found all over the country. You are almost as likely to come across an example in a church in Hertfordshire as you are on the Thames estuary or the outskirts of Dover. Ship graffiti has been found in churches as far inland as Leicestershire and Warwickshire, places where it would actually be very difficult to get any further away from the coast. While it was once argued that these inland examples of ship graffiti actually showed river-going craft rather than sea-going ships, produced in an age when rivers formed a vital part of our inland transport system, such arguments now appear without foundation.

One of the most striking aspects of ship graffiti is that, wherever they are located, in deepest Leicestershire or in view of the south coast, they all appear to depict these vessels in an uncannily similar way. Almost without exception, the ships recorded in a medieval setting are shown as single-masted ships, most often with a masthead or crow's nest, with their sails furled and, as often as not, with clearly depicted anchors lowered. The presence of the masthead is particularly important, it being most usually only found on sea-going vessels rather than their smaller river-based counterparts. Another striking aspect of how these ship images are actually drawn is that they are almost always shown in profile, showing the full hull of the ship as viewed from the side. In essence, rather than being drawn from the waterline upwards, as would be most likely if you were sketching a vessel from life, or as they are often shown in paintings and medieval manuscripts, the ships are depicted as they would only have been seen when first built, or drawn up for repairs. They are, rather oddly, shown in a manner in which most people would only very rarely have seen them. There are a few exceptions to this, such as the late medieval North Sea trading vessel, known as a cog, etched into the walls of the church of Cley Next The Sea, but such exceptions only go to highlight the rather odd way in which the majority of the other ships are depicted.

Although most of the graffiti depicts the ships in an almost identical manner, the quality of the images can vary enormously – quite often within the same building. Generally, most of the examples that have been recorded so far are really quite crude. A few lines outline the hull and mast, with simple cross-hatching for rigging and down strokes outlining the furled sails. The anchors are often no more than a crude cross with a barbed curve attached, roughly tied to the bow of the ship by a single line meant to represent the rope. Indeed, in some cases, the images are so crude as to leave the viewer questioning whether they are actually looking at a ship at all. In their simplest form, such as some of those seen at Blakeney, the whole ship can be shown as no more than three or four lines hastily scratched into the stonework.

At the other end of the spectrum, some of the ships can be shown as elaborately as they would have been in any fine medieval manuscript, complete with detailed rigging layouts and sail plans, planking along the hull, stern decoration and, in a good number of examples, with the crew still aboard. The elegant late-medieval or Tudor vessel etched into the stonework of Bassingham church in Lincolnshire appears to show detailed hull decoration, early gun ports and a high level of detail concerning the way the ship was rigged, which in turn can tell us a great deal about how she was probably sailed. Indeed, the Bassingham ship is so detailed that it could almost have sailed straight out of a medieval manuscript, or have appeared alongside the *Mary Rose* in one of Henry VIII's ship inventories. Similarly, the barrel-shaped hull of the detailed fifteenth-century ship from Norwich Cathedral, with its slightly raised stern and copious rigging lines running to the rear of the ship, echo the illustrations of North Sea trading ships of the late Middle Ages found in manuscripts, stained glass and woodcarving all across northern Europe.

However, the majority of examples of ship graffiti, such as those found at St Margaret's at Cliffe, near Dover, sit happily in the middle ground. They include fairly generic details of the hull design, rigging, sails and anchors that can potentially tell us a great deal about the ships they are meant to portray, but they are certainly no great works of art. At Parham in Suffolk are several examples of what may well be representations of fourteenth-century ships. These too are quite crudely drawn out, but even these rather rough sketches show that the ships had built-up 'castles' at both the bow and stern. They also include rough lines that show the hull planking, suggesting that they may have been clinker built, where the hull planks overlap each other rather than butt together to form a smooth surface. However, at both Parham and St Margaret's at Cliffe, despite being many miles apart from each other, all the ships show with sails furled and at anchor.

The creation of ship graffiti did not stop with the Reformation. Like many other types of church graffiti, they continued to be created almost until the present day. However, the ship graffiti of more recent centuries tends to be relatively rare and confined to certain hotspots around our coast. Churches such as that at Salthouse on the north Norfolk coast can boast of an impressive collection of ship graffiti from the seventeenth and eighteenth centuries. Carved through the red and green pigment on the back of the church rood screen, these ships differ in a number of ways from their medieval counterparts. Most obviously, they are not now found associated with any area of the church that might have been spiritually more significant, and they appear to show large multi-masted vessels that would have been largely alien to these small coastal communities. They appear to be more memorial in nature, recording ships that may have passed through the rapidly silting Norfolk harbour, or lain at anchor off the coast, rather than the ships sailed by local mariners about their everyday tasks. These post-medieval ships are also not only to be found in churches. Some of the finest and most detailed examples have been recorded at sites such as the Tudor House in Southampton, where an English galleon from the late sixteenth century is shown with her decks crowded with armed men and with her gun ports open and ready for action. At Dover Castle, a similarly warlike vessel is to be found etched into the stonework of one of the towers. Dating from the reign of Henry VIII, the graffiti apparently shows an English galleass, a rare hybrid between a galleon and a galley that never found popularity with the Tudor navy, and was eventually deemed unsuitable for military actions outside the Mediterranean.

Although it is interesting to note the wide variety of ships shown, and to note too their distribution patterns across the countryside and the centuries, it does still leave one of the most important questions relating to them unanswered: Why ships? What is the reason, or reasons, that the congregation of many dozens of medieval parish churches felt the need to inscribe images of ships into the fabric of the building? Are these simply images and sketches of an important economic asset that played a major role in virtually every individual's life or, do they have a deeper meaning, significance and function? Are we seeing simple doodles or, perhaps, actual devotion? Once again, there is no single or completely straightforward answer.

In many cases, such as the fragmented remains of the medieval ships on the tower arch at St Mary's, Troston, it is difficult to draw any real conclusions. Surrounded and overwritten by a mass of later graffiti, much of it from the period of the English Civil War, the Troston graffiti ships could have been put there for a whole variety of reasons. They are clearly meant to represent sea-going vessels, despite the church being many dozens of miles inland, but little more than that can be agreed upon. Divorced from their original context by the later graffiti and, sadly, defaced, they hold no real clues as to why they were made. Although much of the surrounding graffiti may appear to have spiritual significance, the same conclusions can't be applied to them. They are medieval ships on a medieval church wall, and everyone and anyone from the rector and choirboys to the lowliest peasant could have been responsible for their creation. However, there are a number of churches where the ship graffiti, and the patterns of its distribution throughout the building, may begin to suggest that there was far more to the creation of these images than the random doodles of choirboys, or the thwarted wanderlust of a country parish priest.

It is worth remembering that ships and ship images were no strangers to the inside of the churches of medieval England. The name of the main public area of the church, the nave, was actually derived directly from the Latin term *navis*, meaning 'ship' or 'vessel', and references dating back to the very earliest days of the Christian church direct that churches should be built long . . . so it will be like a ship. As early as the fourth century, the role of bishop is described as being like one that is a commander of a great ship, and that of deacon as being like the mariners and managers of the ship. While the church itself might have been likened to a ship, it also contained numerous ship images, from those contained in medieval wall paintings (especially the ever-popular St Christopher) to those accompanying the images and statues of the saints. Last, and perhaps most obviously, many English churches actually had detailed models of ships hanging from the intricately carved timbers of the roof.

Often known today as 'church ships', these models were made as votive offerings to the church – often in thanksgiving for a safe return from a perilous journey – and were once a common sight in them up and down the country. The most obvious manifestation of these today are the more than nine hundred examples of model ships, of various ages, that can be seen displayed in the churches of Denmark. These often beautifully built and detailed models were sometimes presented to the church by ship's captains upon retirement, or upon the decommissioning of a vessel or, in a few recorded cases, as thanksgivings for passing through a dangerous storm by a grateful crew. These church ships are not confined to Denmark and, like the ship graffiti itself, are to be found as far away as Spain and Portugal and the Americas. Although very few English examples survive, there are a few sites at which they can still be seen, most notably at All Hallows by the Tower in London, which contains beautifully made examples dating from the eighteenth and nineteenth centuries. The earliest surviving church ships are believed to be several mid-sixteenth-century examples in Portugal. Their relationship to ship graffiti is unclear, but it is worth noting that they, too, show the full hull of the ship, rather than just the section above the waterline.

Although there are no surviving medieval examples, there are a number of early written references that suggest that the practice was widely carried out in England at least as far back as the thirteenth century. In 1227, Henry III instructed that a silver model of his 'great ship' be conveyed to the Norfolk Abbey of Bromholm – site of the Rood of Bromholm, a miracle-working cross that became the site of popular pilgrimage for several centuries – as a thanksgiving gift. As well as those made as offerings within parish churches, these model ships appear to have been popular items for pilgrims, perhaps following the lead of Henry III, to give as gifts at the great shrines of medieval England. Images of shrines exist that show numerous ship models hung around the main reliquary of the saint, and several written accounts mention them. Although it appears that all of these early church ships were swept away, with so much else, at the time of the Reformation, they clearly demonstrate that the presence of ships within churches was commonplace and that these medieval ships often had a meaning and function far beyond a simple wish to record the vessels that may have sat at anchor in a nearby harbour.

In the far east of England, lying upon the north Norfolk coast, stand the four medieval churches that today form the majority of the benefice known as the Glaven parishes. The churches of Cley, Blakeney, Wiveton and Salthouse once served the four intermingled and close-tied communities that surrounded the mouth of the slow-flowing River Glaven and the bustling port that developed at the river's mouth during the Middle Ages. This port – which once brought pilgrims within a stone's throw of the famous shrine of Our Lady at Walsingham, landed North Sea cod and herring by the ton and saw the import of shiploads of Baltic timber – is now all but gone, gradually ruined by long centuries of the silt that choked the harbour of its trade and commerce. However, the four great churches still stand and bear witness to the thriving and multi-cultural community that once filled their naves with worshippers and, more interestingly, covered their walls with graffiti.

Recent studies and detailed surveys have shown that these four churches contain a vast amount of graffiti from the medieval and immediate post-medieval periods. Although, as we have seen, graffiti is not uncommon within medieval churches, the sheer quantity that survives in the churches of the Glaven ports really does make them stand out from the crowd. Exactly why this should be so, remains something of a mystery. The diversity of the graffiti contained within these churches is also quite staggering. Merchant's marks, illuminated capitals, prayers and symbols have all been identified etched into the pale stone of the walls. One piece of graffiti at Wiveton church appears to show a highly detailed depiction of a late-sixteenth-century galleon of three masts, complete with decorated hull, rigging and masthead pennants. However, among the most notable examples of medieval graffiti are those located in the church of St Nicholas at Blakeney, where dozens of little ship engravings sail across the pillars of the south arcade.

Blakeney church has been examined in great detail by leading local historian John Peake, who has been looking at the medieval graffiti found in the local churches for almost a decade. At present, Peake has discovered more than thirty individual ship images within Blakeney church. The images vary greatly in quality and the manner in which they are shown. Some are etched deep into the stonework, making them relatively easy to identify, while others are little more than scratches upon the surface that appear and disappear as the angle of the light shifts throughout the day. Unlike most ship graffiti found throughout England, those from Blakeney show a number of very distinctive and peculiar differences that are not seen elsewhere. The most obvious is that many of the normally single-masted ships are shown with what appears to be a second tiny mast located at the bow or stern of the vessel. The sail is obviously too small to be of much practical use in powering the ship, but it has been suggested that these small sails may have been used by local medieval fishing vessels, used to keep the boat moving slowly forward when using large nets. Given that the Glaven port was famous for the number of ships that were involved in the fishing industry – many of which sailed each summer to catch cod in the North Atlantic waters off Greenland – the depictions of fishing vessels is more than likely, and this strange extra mast may well be a variation peculiar to the north Norfolk coast.

The most fascinating aspect of the ship graffiti at Blakeney lies not with the ships themselves but the way in which they are distributed across the walls of the church. Although graffiti has been found throughout the church, all of the medieval ship images are to be found located upon the pillars of the south arcade. More interestingly still, the ships appear to focus upon one particular area of the south arcade. The pier at the western end contains only two or three examples but, as you move towards the east end of the aisle, the number of little ships increases until, on the final pier, over twenty ships are to be found. Each ship appears to respect the space of those around it, with no two inscriptions obviously overlapping each other. Where two large ships cover a single face of the pillar, smaller later examples nestle between them, making the most of the space left to them – but never crossing over those that came before.

This ship-covered pier is directly opposite a now-empty image niche and lies close to the position of the former aisle altar, suggesting that the graffiti is linked to these areas. The other remarkable observation concerning the Blakeney ships is that, although they are difficult to see today, when first created they would have been very visible indeed. Examination has shown that during the Middle Ages, the piers were painted a deep red colour, most probably a locally produced red-ochre pigment. A lack of this pigment within the lines of the graffiti itself indicates that they were scratched through the red paint to expose the pale stone beneath. The result would have been striking. A deep red sea crowded with small white ships. The question must be, why should this be so? Why are all these little ships clustered in this one area of the church, around the image niche and side altar? Why was this particular area of the church deemed suitable, or even appropriate, for this kind of activity? The answer may well lie in the traditional layout of the medieval church, which was fairly formulaic. The chancel and high altar lay at the eastern end, with the tower at the west. On the north side was often to be found the Mary altar or, in larger and richer churches, a Lady chapel, dedicated to the Virgin Mary. However, if a church had a south aisle, then there was most usually another altar at its east end. Although this altar could have multiple dedications, and could even be the spiritual home of local trade or church guilds, it was often dedicated to the church's own patron, or dedicatory, saint. In the case of Blakeney, this side altar is today dedicated to St Michael, but the church itself is dedicated to St Nicholas, and it is quite likely that this side altar was also once similarly dedicated.

These days, St Nicholas is best known for his association with children and the Christmas festivities. However, during the Middle Ages, he was also widely thought of as the patron saint of those in peril upon the sea, after having reputedly calmed a storm by calling upon God's aid, and thereby saving both himself and the crew of the ship in which he was travelling. The cult of St Nicholas appears to have been fairly widespread, with many churches on the coast and in port towns being dedicated to the saint. The Blakeney graffiti, clustered around an area that was probably once associated with St Nicholas, suggests that these images may well have been directly related to the saint and his cult. The most obvious conclusion is that these images were created as an act of devotion over a period of time. Prayers, perhaps, from those whose loved ones were in peril upon the sea? A thank-you for a safe journey undertaken, or a plea for safe passage on journeys yet to come? The most striking feature about these graceful acts of devotion is that they are very clearly personal intercessions – which did not require the involvement of pope, bishop or priest – between the congregation and the very fabric of the church building. Designed to be visible to all, but a personal and intimate plea between the artist and their God.

The link between ship graffiti and St Nicholas is not simply limited to the church at Blakeney, and the same distribution patterns are to be seen elsewhere. On the south coast of England sits the beautiful medieval town of Winchelsea, or 'New Winchelsea' as it was often known (the old Winchelsea, originally lying nearer the coast, having been swept away by a great storm in the early Middle Ages). In the centre of the medieval planned town is the great church of St Thomas, originally built on the scale of a small cathedral; though today, little more than the chancel and eastern sections of the aisles survive. Despite having lost much of the original church, what remains is still the size of the average parish church, and is covered in early-graffiti inscriptions. Like Blakeney, the entire building has many early-graffiti inscriptions etched into just about every available surface, including the nationally important tomb effigies for which the church is justly famous. Among the mass of ritual protection marks, names and dates are also to be found a number of ship graffiti. However, all these ships can be found on one particular pillar, that located at the eastern end of the north arcade, opposite the entrance to a side chapel – which the church records show was once dedicated to St Nicholas.

The link between ships and St Nicholas is also to be seen in numerous other medieval churches around the country. A few miles down the coast from Winchelsea can be found the ancient church of St Nicholas at 'Brighthelmstone', or Brighton as it is better known today, with its beautifully decorated twelfth-century font. Carved from imported Caen stone, the font shows four separate scenes, one of which is clearly part of the legend of St Nicholas and depicts a single-masted sailing ship that contains many of the elements usually found in ship graffiti. Back in Norfolk, at the once bustling seaport of King's Lynn, stands the imposing Chapel of St Nicholas. Although not an actual parish church, the chapel was first built in the middle of the twelfth century, then rebuilt in the late fourteenth century to act as a subsidiary chapel to the town church. It was constructed on a monumental scale, largely with money donated by the town's wealthy merchant class, and remains the largest chapel of ease anywhere in the country. The merchants of King's Lynn had made their money in trade from the sea and St Nicholas would have been an obvious saint to appeal to. As a result, the building was once home to a great deal of ship imagery. An elaborately carved medieval bench end, created as part of the later rebuilding and now in the Victoria and Albert museum, is regarded as one of the finest wood-carvings of a ship to survive from the period – and it wasn't just the timbers that contained images of ships. The south porch still contains at least one example of late-medieval ship graffiti, as well as several beautifully incised merchant's marks, suggesting that the links between the merchants and their devotion to St Nicholas remained strong for many centuries.

The links between ship graffiti and St Nicholas are strong at a number of sites, but they certainly don't explain all the examples that have been discovered. There are too many churches where ship graffiti can be found that have no obvious connections to either the sea or a St Nicholas cult, suggesting that there is rather a lot more going on than a simple saintly cult. And even where a St Nicholas connection can be shown to have existed, this still doesn't actually explain the meaning behind the inscriptions. Recently, it has been suggested that many of the ships look as though they have been damaged in some way, with sails missing and yardarms torn away, so each of these little carved ships may well represent a ship that never came back, a ship that was lost for ever to the storms and the sea. At sites like Blakeney, where dozens of ships still sail across the church walls, the sheer numbers of ship images present may make this appear unlikely. However, when you consider that the Blakeney graffiti was created over several centuries, and that each ship graffiti may only represent a loss every couple of years, the numbers soon become, if not acceptable, at least realistic.

While such nice simple explanations may be attractive to archaeologists and historians, it is rarely the case when the evidence is examined. It is more likely that there were several different reasons behind the creation of the ship graffiti that now litters the walls of our parish churches. The links between ships and travel have always been strong, and were never stronger than during the Middle Ages, when a journey by ship was likely to be one of the most hazardous undertakings an individual could make. Perhaps these images, rather than being specific to one particular cult, are more general in nature? Perhaps they hark back to the origins of Christianity itself, and the imagery of the 'ship of the church'? We can suggest a number of theories that might pass as explanations – but certainty died with the people who actually created the images. What we can say with any sense of certainty is that for the people who created these images, for the individuals who spent hours carving them into the stonework of their parish church, they had both meaning and function. They represented the very real hopes, dreams and fears of those who came before us.

If we drained the world's oceans, pushed the water back from the coast, to see what really lies beneath, how many shattered wrecks would we find? How many fragments of broken ships, broken lives and broken communities scatter the seabed? The thin clear line of the ocean horizon would be replaced by the upstanding, jagged and broken teeth of a graveyard of rotten timbers and sea-bleached bone. Our seas are grave-yards bigger than those of the largest cathedrals, dotted with the unblessed graves of a million fathers, husbands and brothers. Each single loss, each upstanding wreck, represents a life ended and the lives of those left behind shattered and altered in ways that they never imagined. In a single storm, a single night of foul weather and high water, many individual worlds were dashed upon unseen rocks. Perhaps, then, the ships that still sail sedately across the walls of our medieval churches represent more than just images of pretty medieval vessels? Perhaps each one represents something more: each one, a silent prayer made solid in stone.

CHAPTER ELEVEN

MEN OF THE STONES: ARCHITECTURAL INSCRIPTIONS

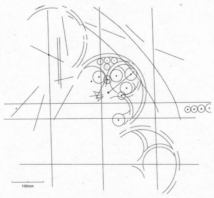

Architectural design from the rear of the rood screen, Caston, Norfolk

'In England it is very evident that the earliest churches were humble structures, suitable to the means and tastes of a people but just emerging from barbarism'

Rev. G. S. Tyack, Lore and Legend of the English Church, 1899

The medieval craftsmen who constructed the thousands of beautiful churches that still scatter the English countryside left behind more than their personal mason's marks: in rare cases, they also left behind details of how these buildings were actually designed and built. While a very few master masons left fragments of design in medieval manuscripts, now safely stored away in archives and museums, others left their work upon the very walls of the churches themselves. Working sketches, architectural designs and builders' calculations created by medieval masons are among the very rarest inscriptions to be found in English churches, and they certainly rank alongside the most fascinating. Though they are not what we would technically think of as graffiti, these inscriptions offer us insights into areas of the past that we simply cannot find elsewhere; they let us view and understand the creative processes that went into the designing of more than ten thousand medieval masterpieces in stone.

The manuscript evidence that survives concerning the design of medieval churches and cathedrals is scant, to say the very least. The earliest manuscript design known is that for Strasbourg Cathedral, which is one of a series of drawings created for the committee responsible for the building fabric, and appears to date back to about 1250. Other similar designs, which are really more artist's impressions of how the finished work would look than full building schematics, survive for Vienna, Ulm and Clermont-Ferrand. All of these surviving drawings are highly detailed works of art but give little detail that would have been of use to the masons working on the project. They were designed to show how the finished work would look, in the hope that those responsible for paying for the actual work would commission that particular design. Given that there are marked differences in detail between the drawings of Strasbourg and the finished cathedral, it is safe to assume that these were also discussion documents, destined to be altered, changed and amended as the client saw fit. This is made clear by the survival of a contract for the building of the cloister portal of the Hospital of St Jacques in Paris. Dated to 1474, it was made by stonecutter Guillaume Monnin, outlining the work that was to be undertaken, and included a small architectural drawing to allow the hospital governors to judge the final appearance of the proposed work. No such large-scale medieval architectural drawings are known to have survived for any similar buildings in England.

Alongside these artists impressions of how a finished building was meant to look, there are a few other documents that relate to the building of medieval churches and cathedrals. The first are a number of actual building contracts that have survived to the present day. These are invariably for the larger abbeys and cathedrals such as Beverley and York Minsters, where records of significant building works, and the financial outlay it entailed, have survived far better than those for the smaller parish churches. Some of these contracts do include a good deal of detail about what was expected from the master mason; such as that drawn up in 1261 between Martin de Lonay and the abbot of Saint-Gilles-du-Gard, which stipulated what de Lonay was paid, when he was to turn up for work and how much he was to be reimbursed for living expenses – but contains little more than the barest of outlines as to what the building itself was to be like. Perhaps of more interest is the thirteenth-century notebook of Villard de Honnecourt. He was not, as far as we can understand it, an actual mason or architect, but rather someone fascinated by design and buildings. His notebook, which is rather a collection of drawings and sketches, states that 'in this book you will find advice on buildings in stone, on machines used in carpentry, on the art of portrait, on drawing and on the art of geometry'. To satisfy his curiosity, he travelled between a number of sites where major cathedral projects were underway, including Reims, Lausanne and Chartres, and here he copied down details of the masons' work, including designs for rose windows, profiles of moulded decoration and sketches of elevations under construction. While de Honnecourt's sketches have been shown to be by no means highly accurate, their value lies in the light they shed on the actual construction and design process. However, despite the details that can be highlighted by all these surviving documents, none really gives a great deal of insight into how the medieval craftsmen went about taking an artistic drawing on vellum and creating a three-dimensional cathedral or church in stone; for that we must look to the walls.

Until very recently, it was believed that fewer than twenty early architectural inscriptions survived anywhere in England. However, recent research and systematic surveys of medieval-graffiti inscriptions have identified many previously unknown examples, almost doubling the number of known survivals, and more come to light each passing year. Given that many areas of England and Wales have yet to be systematically surveyed, it is quite likely that there are many more of these inscriptions still awaiting discovery. One of the main reasons that so few of these type of inscriptions have been discovered until recent years is that many of them tend to be created on quite a large scale, meaning that a cursory glance at a wall may reveal only a few seemingly meaningless lines and curves. It is only when the whole surface of the wall is looked at that it becomes apparent that these lines and curves are part of a far larger architectural design.

The inscriptions found to date can vary enormously. At Byland Abbey in North Yorkshire, designs relating the great rose window, dating to the very early thirteenth century, were found on both a floor slab and on one wall. Further south, at Christchurch Priory in Hampshire, a design for a tracery window dating to the late thirteenth century were discovered on a wall. The design, which was created to actual size, would have been used by the mason to work out the construction details needed for such a complex design. However, not all architectural designs were created on such a monumental scale. At Weston Longville in Norfolk, two inscriptions were discovered lightly etched into the pillars of the south arcade that appeared to show designs for tracery windows. Set out with compasses and straight edges, at least one of the designs appears to relate to a window that still exists on the south side of the chancel. Although neither sketch could be called a finished and complete design, they look as though they were working drawings where the mason was putting together the basic elements of the tracery pattern and working out the main principles of construction. Both inscriptions were clearly created in situ and both were only about 140mm across, allowing them to fit neatly on a single face of the pillar. An almost identical design to one of those discovered at Weston Longville was also found high up on a pillar at Holy Trinity church in Dartford, Kent, which can only have been produced by a mason already working from a ladder or scaffold.

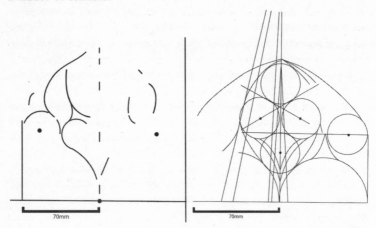

A pair of architectural designs for tracery windows, Weston Longville, Norfolk

Many of the architectural designs that have been found appear quite clearly to be either unfinished or to only show part of a design; in some cases, the most technically difficult sections. At Leighton Buzzard church in Bedfordshire, there are two very complex and beautiful designs for elaborate church windows. One is for a circular window, similar to a rose window, and the other is a more traditional tracery design for an arched window. Both appear to be complete designs but, if you look closely at that for the arched window, it soon becomes obvious that the lower section of the design, showing the glazed vertical openings, is in no way inscribed with the same precision as the upper section. It would appear that someone, perhaps at the time or perhaps many years later, saw the unfinished window design on the wall and decided that they would finish the job themselves. At several other sites, small drawings that are clearly the work of masons or their apprentices show only the briefest outlines of proposed designs. In the Surrey churches of Banstead and Pyrford, simple outlines of arched windows and basic tracery are to be found on the pillars, while at Scole church in Norfolk, the lines of a geometric tracery window are still to be seen etched into the stonework. Although window designs are certainly prominent among these inscriptions, they are by no means the only designs that the masons left etched into the walls. At Sawston church in Cambridgeshire, a design for some sort of moulding profile is etched into one of the pillars. The design is now quite badly eroded and it is difficult to understand whether it was a design for part of a moulding that still exists within the church, or perhaps just a speculative outline laid down by the mason planning future projects.

Not all of these architectural inscriptions are to be found on stonework – one of the most fruitful areas of searching has been the back of church rood screens. These screens, designed to separate the nave from the chancel, were most usually highly decorated on the side that faced the nave. Often, images of the saints were created in immense detail, highlighted with gold leaf and picked out in expensive pigments. Although many of these screens were swept away at the time of the Reformation – and those that did survive were badly defaced by iconoclasts – enough survive in areas such as Devon and East Anglia to have been the subject of numerous studies over the years. However, in terms of architectural designs, it isn't the splendid western face of the rood screens that are of interest but the plain eastern face; that which faced into the chancel. It is upon this face of the screen that several detailed architectural designs have recently been discovered. At Colton in Norfolk, a complex design has been recorded, again created in situ, that appears to relate to the design of the upper section of the screen itself. This is of particular interest as nobody now knows exactly what the upper section originally looked like, it having been sawn off and destroyed during the Reformation in the mid-sixteenth century. However, the design on the rear of the screen is detailed enough to allow a full reconstruction of the upper section to be attempted. At Blythburgh in Suffolk, a similarly detailed architectural inscription was discovered on the rear of the parclose screen that may well be the design for the vaulting that once supported the canopy that ran along the length of the top of the screen. At Belaugh church in the Norfolk Broads, in a reversal of what might be seen as normal practice, multiple architectural inscriptions that appear to relate to the making of the upper section of the rood screen are to be found inscribed into the stonework of the piers, rather suggesting that the carpenters who built the screen did most of the work on site, rather than, as has often been thought, in a remote workshop.

All these designs can tell us a good deal about the individual churches in which they were found. They can also tell us a good deal about the practical design process of the medieval craftsmen who built and fitted out these churches, and in some cases – as at Colton – then can reveal aspects of the building's history that have long been thought lost for ever. In some very special and unusual cases, these architectural designs can also shed light on the development of architectural styles in England, and offer an immediate and personal insight to events that reverberated far beyond the walls of a single church, priory or abbey.

In the quiet and secluded village of Binham, a few miles inland from the north Norfolk coast, stand the remains of a once-magnificent medieval priory. The priory was originally established as an outlying cell of the great monastery of St Alban and had a chequered history, being at one point besieged, and at another seen as a refuge for monks who had lost their wits and needed to be secluded deep in the East Anglian countryside. The priory was also frequented by pilgrims making their way to the nearby shrine of Our Lady at Walsingham, and contained its own small shrine dedicated to the pious healer, Sir John Schorne. Although most of the priory complex was lost at the Reformation – sold off to wealthy landowners who left little but jumbled stones – the whole of the western end of the priory church was saved and adopted as the local parish church. Today, the site welcomes thousands of visitors a year to its peaceful surroundings, and the busy congregation hosts numerous musical and dramatic events in the church and priory grounds, returning life to a most beautiful site that was once almost lost for ever. However, Binham Priory's main claim to fame has nothing to do with pilgrims, sieges or mad monks, but rather that it was here, at this remote church in forgotten north Norfolk, that an architectural revolution began.

The fact that there is something very different about Binham's architecture strikes you as soon as you walk inside the nave of the surviving section of the priory church. At the eastern end of what is left of the original church, the nave rises in three tiers – arcade, gallery and clerestory – in what can best be described as Romanesque semi-circular arches. However, as your eyes move towards the western end of the church, you will note a clear and distinct change in the style, a clear break in the fabric, after which the Romanesque arches give way to the shallow pointed arches of the early Gothic period: on the south side, only the last arch of the arcade is Gothic; at gallery level, the last two arches; and at clerestory, the last three – the combined effect creating a staggered break across the building that jars the eye and makes it appear that the remains of two once-magnificent medieval churches have been inexpertly glued together. Quite simply, this entire priory was built at a time of change and transition, when the older Romanesque style was being replaced by the new imported Gothic style; and with building work already almost complete, the builders adopted the new style as they went. Despite the odd quirkiness of the half-finished, twice-built nave, Binham's real claim to fame lies in the revolutionary design of the west front.

According to the St Albans-based medieval chronicler Matthew Paris, the west front of Binham Priory was built during the administration of Prior Richard de Parco in about 1245. Even today, the casual observer can see that it was a work of superb quality, equal to the very best mason's work being undertaken anywhere in England at that time. However, it is the windows inserted into the west front that make it so very special. The great west window and the two small windows at the western end of both of the aisles are the very earliest recorded examples of the use of Gothic 'bar tracery' anywhere in England. It really doesn't sound like too much of a big deal when you see it written down before you, but it is important to understand what this small change in design meant for architecture throughout England.

Prior to the introduction of bar tracery, windows in churches, abbeys and cathedrals had been created using a construction technique known as 'plate tracery'. At its most basic, the general idea was that if you wanted to put a window into a building, then you first built a wall and then cut a hole in it. Essentially, this is what you are seeing when you look at the small lancet-style windows in any very early church, and the problems are obvious. If you cut too big a hole in the wall, you will weaken the wall to such an extent that it will collapse. However, as churches grew bigger, there was a need for more light and bigger windows. The first answer to this problem was to group sets of lancets, or openings, together, cutting them through a thinner section of the wall (the 'plate'). Although this did allow larger windows to be created, it was still subject to the same limitations, with window size being finely balanced against the subsequent loss in structural strength of the wall. However, the development of bar tracery in twelfth-century France changed everything. The new style involved inserting carefully cut and intertwined stone mullions into the window space. Not only were these stonework spiders' webs highly decorative, they were also designed to be structural. In essence, the bar tracery *added* to the strength of the wall rather than diminished it, and windows could suddenly become far taller and wider than they had ever been before – and without the danger of the wall in which they were inserted suddenly collapsing.

The introduction of bar tracery paved the way for a revolution in church architecture across western Europe. Without it, we would never have seen the great cathedrals of light and glass at sites such as Lincoln, Westminster Abbey, York Minster and Norwich. This new building style allowed for massive windows, delicate walls of glass, arcades reaching towards the heavens – and it all began in a sleepy little village in north Norfolk. The great west window of Binham Priory was the very first example of this new style to be used in England, and pre-dates its use at Westminster Abbey by as much as a decade. Just why it came first to Binham has never really been satisfactorily explained. Some claim that the priory patron, recently returned from exile in France, had seen the new style being built at sites such as Reims and wanted to emulate it. Others suggest that it may have been the work of a visiting French master mason, looking for new clients on this side of the Channel. Whatever the truth of the matter, what is significant is that the first steps on the road to the Gothic revolution took place here.

While everyone agrees that Binham was the first site to actually use bar tracery in England, that is about as far as the general consensus on the building's architecture goes. Indeed, over the last century, the west window of the priory has found itself the subject of a continuing debate between architectural historians, a debate that at times has become rather heated. The debate is centred around one seemingly rather simple question: Was the window when originally built a four-light' or an eight-light window? The lights of a window are merely the spaces between the stone mullions that make up the tracery pattern itself. While this might seem, to non-architectural historians, a rather small and petty point, it has far greater implications. If the window at Binham, so the argument goes, was of four lights, then it can be seen as a simple and evolutionary step forward in the long development of window styles, towards the sublime perfection found at sites like Westminster Abbey. However, if the window was actually of eight lights, then it must be regarded as more of a revolutionary leap forward in its own right. The argument, you would think, would be simple to solve; just look at the window itself. However, today, the great window is almost completely bricked up, having been seen to be failing and in danger of collapse in the late eighteenth century, and the only two early prints made before the failure appear to directly contradict one another. Both prints, actually showing very little detail, appear to support the different sides in the argument, with one clearly showing four lights and the other eight. In recent years, it is the more conservative of the architectural historians, those who believe in the four-light theory, that appear to be in the ascendant, with the eight-light theory being so unfashionable as to even have been termed in one scholarly publication as a 'myth'.

The answer to these arguments turned out to be rather closer to hand at Binham than the architectural historians could have possibly imagined. Survey work at the priory in 2010 revealed the presence of a number of previously overlooked large-scale inscriptions etched into the stonework of the church pillars. Eventually, it was found that there were at least five separate inscriptions scattered around the western end of the nave, and tantalising suggestions that there had once been other examples present, too. Such large-scale inscriptions are a rarity, and to find this many within one building was unheard of in England. The question, though, was what exactly did they relate to, and at what date were they created? Despite the fact that most of the inscriptions were extremely badly worn and eroded, it turned out that giving these architectural designs a general date was far easier than is usually the case with early inscriptions. They had been inscribed into stonework that, everyone agreed, had been finished at some point in the twelfth century, and yet were still partially covered over by a medieval paint scheme from the late thirteenth or early fourteenth century, meaning that they had to have been created at some point between those two dates. Detailed research into the best surviving inscription found that it appeared to show part of the design for the great west window, suggesting that it had actually been created by the master mason responsible back in about 1245. What is more, the design suggested that the original window was an eight-light one rather than one of four lights. The discovery sparked a whole new round of research into the history of the priory, unearthing new images and woodcuts that also seemed to support the idea – previously almost unthinkable – that the window was indeed of a revolutionary eight-light design.

But what of the mason, the man himself? Who was this individual who inscribed an architectural revolution into the walls of the priory, inscriptions have now long outlived the window that he built? A few things can be learned from the inscriptions themselves. We know, for instance, from the way he drew the great sweeping curves across the surface, pressing harder in some parts than in others, that he was probably right-handed. The fact that the designs themselves appear to be working drawings – schematics working out new ideas from first principles – suggests he was unlikely to have been a highly experienced imported French mason who had worked on similar Gothic sites abroad. Indeed, the inscriptions appear very much to suggest that the designs were being worked out by trial and error. They are not the beautifully coloured final drawings that survive for sites such as Strasbourg Cathedral, but represent an intermediate stage in the design process; the moment when ideas are translated into a workable reality. Here, in a small Norfolk Priory, one man stood facing this very same wall, dividers and straight-edge in hand, and puzzled his way through an architectural maze. To know that he found a solution, you need only turn your back to the wall and admire the sweeping curves of the arcade that still stands to this day, a testament to a man whose name we will never know.

CHAPTER TWELVE

THE CHIVALRIC CODE: HERALDIC GRAFFITI

A graffiti rose, Lindsey, Suffolk

*'. . . and the children of Israel . . . pitched by their standards,
and so they set forward, every one after their families,
according to the house of their fathers'*

Numbers, 2:34

Today, most people probably believe themselves to be pretty familiar with the concept of heraldry. It has been argued that its origins can be traced back to the standards of the Roman legions that once marched across Europe, with echoes that continued throughout the Dark Ages in the tribal symbols of the ruling Anglo-Saxon houses: the wild boars of Mercia and the wolves of the East Anglians once used as decoration and helmet crests. Yet, it really isn't until after the Norman Conquest that heraldry, in a form that we would recognise today, begins to emerge.

The general concept of heraldry is a simple one. It means a symbol, banner or coat of arms that can be recognised by all – friends, followers or enemies – in the chaos and hurly burly of a medieval battle; a distinct achievement, associated with only one individual or household that marked friend from foe. However, as with most modern views of the medieval world, this idea is now considered somewhat simplistic. What may have begun as a simple scheme of identification evolved into an intricate and multi-layered language that, at its most complex, was largely understandable only to the expert. And like other languages, it too developed, diversified and diverged so that, by the later Middle Ages and post-medieval periods, heraldry bore as little resemblance to its early Norman antecedents as the spoken Middle English of Geoffrey Chaucer did to the old tongue of the Anglo-Saxons and Alfred the Great.

By the end of the Middle Ages, heraldry had, at one and the same time, become a far more formalised and institutionalised set of rules and regulations – and a fluid and much slimmed-down collection of fragmented ideas and symbols. At one end of the spectrum, members of the nobility followed strict and enforceable codes that regulated their own heraldry. The simple banners of the early Middle Ages had become complex 'achievements' of arms, including heraldic beasts such as lions, griffins and unicorns as supporters, and elaborate crests that surmounted the shield or helm. The whole system was presided over by the College of Arms and its heralds, who regulated the complex system and, if the need arose, even arbitrated in disputes. At the other end of the spectrum, the nobles' own servants, tenants and followers received 'livery and maintenance'. While the maintenance may well be self-explanatory, basically involving a room-and-board agreement between master and servant, the livery element was often no more than a watered-down element of their own lord's heraldic achievement, which they were expected to wear. For the more important household servants and retainers, the livery might take the form of a jacket or gown in their lord's colours, sometimes including a decorative livery badge in precious metal. For the lower orders, a simple base-metal badge, many of which survive to this day, was far more the norm. In the case of nobles such as Richard, Earl of Gloucester (later Richard III), his followers' livery took the form of a white-boar badge, his own personal symbol that appeared on his banner and as a supporter of his coat of arms. While such liveries were obviously related directly to heraldry, they appear to have been largely unregulated, with nobles changing their own personal badges, and that of their followers, pretty much upon a whim.

The complexities of medieval heraldry, and the medieval system of livery and maintenance, appear in no way simplified when it comes to examining the numerous examples of medieval heraldic graffiti that have been recorded across England. Although it isn't perhaps one of the most common types of early graffiti recorded in medieval churches and chapels, there are enough examples found for it to be considered significant. In addition, it is also one of the very few types of graffiti inscription for which we actually have a written reference.

In the middle years of the fifteenth century, Eton scholar William Wey undertook a pilgrimage to the Holy Land. Such a journey was likely to have been a once-in-a-lifetime experience for those who could afford to make the trip and, for many, the perils were such that it did actually result in their deaths. The hazards were numerous, with everything from the threat of shipwreck and cut-throat bandits at the most extreme, to unscrupulous hostel owners and profiteering local officials, making the whole journey as much a physical trial as it was a spiritual one. As many writers of the period noted, it was a foolish man who undertook such a venture without first making their last will and testament. However, the intrepid William Wey not only undertook the trip, travelling on foot across France and Italy and then via galley from Venice, but has left a fascinatingly detailed account of his journey. Written very much as a guidebook for those who would travel in his footsteps, his account is full of acute observations, sage advice and well-worn anecdotes that continued a tradition of travel guides that was already many centuries old. As well as detailing his own journey, with suggestions as to where the best inns and hostels were located, and where good food could be found at a reasonable price, Wey helpfully records the local customs and regulations applied to Christians wishing to travel in the Muslim-held Middle East. Among these, he states that, upon arrival at the Holy Sepulchre in Jerusalem, where the pilgrims are destined to be locked inside for the night, they are informed that 'on no account are they to inscribe their coats of arms into the walls'.

While Wey's account makes clear that scratching graffiti into the most sacred site in Christendom was not to be encouraged, it also implies that such a regulation was only needed because the practice had become commonplace among visiting western nobles. Similarly, Felix Fabri, another pilgrim who left an account of his visit to the Holy Land, mentions the practice among fellow pilgrims of setting up their own coats of arms in whichever hostel they were staying that night – much to the offence of the local population. The evidence of this graffiti habit by pilgrims can still be seen to this day at a number of sites in the Middle East. The best known of these is probably the ancient monastery of St Catherine in the Sinai, where the coats of arms of many genera-tions of medieval knights and nobles – who travelled there as an exten-sion to their visit to Jerusalem – are deeply etched into the stones and timber of the ancient buildings. Among the coats of arms present are said to be a number of medieval princes, and the arms of Sir John Mandeville, the noted medieval traveller, who journeyed almost as far as Marco Polo (or early author of travel fiction, depending upon which account you believe).

Heraldic-graffiti inscriptions can be found all over England, scratched into church walls such as Worlington in Suffolk and the chapels of fortifications such as Norwich and Carlisle castles. Their quality can be almost as variable as their content. Many are clearly and neatly drawn and obviously meant to portray a recognisable coat of arms, such as that found on the chancel arch of Troston church. Others are so stylised and simplistic that it is difficult to believe that they were ever anything more than generic representations of heraldry. However, in most cases, even with the very best examples of heraldic inscriptions, it has been impossible to identify which family or individual the coats of arms may have belonged to. The reason for this is that heraldry, from no matter what period, is entirely reliant upon colour – which is the one thing rarely found with graffiti inscriptions. Even the most complex heraldic design could, with different colour variations, belong to a number of noble families or individuals, and the wide possible date range of many graffiti inscriptions makes positive identification even harder. For example, the Troston graffiti could potentially represent any one of about half a dozen families from the period between 1400 and 1600, depending upon the intended colour scheme. However, just to make things more confusing still, none of those families have been identified as having had any links with either the parish or the church; the closest being the Thorp (or Thorpe) family from Lincolnshire. And so, while the coats of arms of many long-dead knights may well adorn the walls of our parish churches, their names may never actually be known. The heraldry, once designed to clearly identify them in the heat of battle and represent their own noble heritage, has lost its voice and become silent.

Sixteenth-century Guild mark, Carlisle Cathedral

Large and elaborate compass-drawn design, St Mary's church,
Sedgeford, Norfolk

Medieval painted consecration cross,
St Margaret's church, Lt Dunham, Norfolk

A small selection of crosses discovered in English medieval churches

Compass-drawn
Hexfoil or 'daisy wheel',
All Saint's church,
Barnardiston, Suffolk

A small selection of compass-drawn Hexfoil or 'Daisy Wheel' designs from English medieval churches

Late medieval curse inscription naming the 'Keynfford' family, Norwich Cathedral, Norfolk

Medieval demon inscription complete with flesh-hook, St Mary's church, Beachamwell, Norfolk

Late medieval demon from the east face of the chancel arch, St Mary's church, Troston, Suffolk

Fourteenth or fifteenth
century ship graffiti, St
Margaret's church, Cley
next the Sea, Norfolk

A fine example of late medieval ship graffiti, Norwich Cathedral, Norfolk

A late medieval 'rebus' or puzzle inscription, St Mary's church, Lidgate, Suffolk

A medieval windmill or postmill inscription, St Mary's church, Dalham, Suffolk

Seventeenth century memorial inscriptions, Norwich Cathedral, Norfolk

An unusually deeply cut heraldic inscription, All Saint's church, Worlington, Suffolk

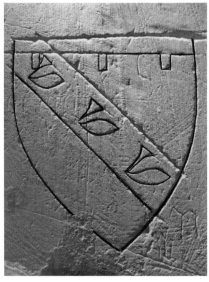

A beautifully executed heraldic inscription from the chancel arch, St Mary's church, Troston, Suffolk

Examples of precisely cut medieval mason's marks found in many of our English parish churches.

Late sixteenth century monogram or merchant's mark, St Mary's church, Westerham, Kent

Figures of medieval singers and musicians, St John the Baptist's church, Stoke by Clare, Suffolk

Figure of a late fourteenth or early fifteenth century knight, St Andrew's church, Weybread, Suffolk

Fifteenth century figure of a man armed with sword and buckler, the church of St Botolph and St John the Baptist, Croxton Kerrial, Leicestershire

Some heraldic graffiti are easier to decipher than others. The examples from Carlisle and Worlington are very well executed, showing enough detail to be able to describe them in full heraldic terms. The Worlington example is particularly fine, showing a lion rampant upon a plain shield, which is repeated twice across the pillars of the church. In addition, the same church contains another shield that may well depict the medieval arms of the city of Jerusalem. Similarly well-executed shield designs can be found at Ludham in Norfolk, albeit located over three metres up on a pillar, and at Shere in Surrey, where multiple examples sit superimposed upon each other. At Anstey in Hertfordshire, at least half a dozen recognisable shields are to be found etched lightly into the stonework, while at Ashton in Northamptonshire, clearly etched heraldic shields are among the most obvious of all the surviving graffiti inscriptions found decorating a medieval tomb.

Having said that, these relatively well-executed and clear heraldic inscriptions are really quite unusual. The vast majority of known examples can, at best, be described as being of rather poor quality. In most cases, the shields show badly drawn examples of what can only be described as generic heraldry. While they are clearly heraldic in nature, they are, just as clearly, not meant to represent the arms of any particular family. Examples from Norfolk sites such as Great Dunham and Swannington, and Great Bardfield and Hatfield Broad Oak in Essex, are so simplistic as to be barely recognisable as shields at all. The question must be, why did someone go to all the bother of creating a shield and heraldry, but do it so poorly that it clearly isn't meant to represent an actual coat of arms? One possible answer is that these shields were just meant to represent all those things that were associated with having a coat of arms, such as knighthood, chivalry and nobility. This in turn rather begs the question of who, then, created these inscriptions? Do they perhaps represent the aspirations of those individuals? Are they, like many of the other graffiti inscriptions recorded in English churches, representing the hopes and dreams of the congregation? If this is the case, and they do represent the ambitions of the person who created them, then why do we not find similar representations of other ambitions – a bigger house, a better cart etc.? Just to further confuse the issue, these simple heraldic designs are also to be found on many pilgrim badges and souvenirs of the period. Invariably mixed with recognisable religious and votive designs, this does rather suggest that the heraldic designs may well have had a religious or spiritual significance. However, just what that significance may have been remains a mystery.

Heraldic graffiti is not confined to the obvious shield designs and coats of arms, but rather falls into two distinct categories. The majority are unquestionably the fairly standard shield shapes. However, there are a significant number that appear to show entire 'achievements' of arms, including helmet crest and supporters. While these are really rather rare, they are fascinating because that additional information should, or could, allow a positive identification. Once again, these type of inscriptions can vary from the very complex, such as those found at Anstey in Hertfordshire, to the simple, such as that excavated from the remains of Bermondsey Abbey in London. The Anstey example, which shows a helmet surmounted by a well-executed horse-head crest, is considered one of the best of its type yet discovered. However, even given the amount of detail shown in the inscription, it has been impossible to tie it down to an individual – leaving Violet Pritchard to fall back on the suggestion that it was probably Continental in origin. The Bermondsey Abbey example is perhaps pretty typical of most of these types of graffiti, showing a shield with a very simple cross motif, a stylised sword crossing behind it and all crowned with a very simplified helmet that may (or may not) show a crest. Like the much simpler depictions of shields alone, these very simple 'achievements' are rather difficult to reconcile with real heraldry. Once again, they would appear to have a function or meaning that is clearly not just to represent the heraldry of a single family or individual. In the same way that shield designs are often seen without helmets and crests above them, so too are helmets that do not appear to accompany a shield design. An elaborate medieval jousting helmet from Fordingbridge in Hampshire, shown in profile and clearly having once sported some sort of crest, sits alone on the stonework with no sign of a shield ever having been present. In such cases, it really isn't clear whether the design was ever meant to truly represent heraldry.

Alongside the more usual coats of arms and shields, there are a number of motifs and symbols that have traditionally been interpreted as being heraldic in nature, but are now open to question. Perhaps the most obvious is the 'ragged staff'. Traditionally associated with the earls of Warwick, the ragged staff was used as a livery badge by the earl's retainers and followers, alongside the more complex 'bear and ragged staff' symbol. Examples of cast lead badges have been discovered in excavations of medieval sites across the country, and it is thought that these were the cheap and mass-produced badges handed out to the earl's lower-class supporters and followers. Numerous examples of the ragged staff have also been found etched into the walls of English parish churches at sites such as Norwich Cathedral, Pyrford, Frostenden in Suffolk, Troston, St Peter Hungate church in Norwich, Anstey and Harlton. In fact, it is now believed that far too many examples have been found etched into church walls.

While the earls of Warwick were undoubtedly popular, the instances of their supposed livery badge being identified in early graffiti is simply too commonplace. Examples have been found all over the country, from Dorset to Norfolk, and from Kent to Northumberland, and invariably in a church setting. While this may not be obviously unusual, what is a little amiss is the fact that the badges of all the other great noble families of the later Middle Ages – the Howards, deVeres, Staffords and Buckinghams etc. – are not. In fact, with the exception of a few dog-like inscriptions, that could in a good light be interpreted as talbots (a type of medieval hunting hound and symbol of the earls of Shrewsbury), the examples of livery badges etched into the walls of English churches are most notable by their absence. Are we, then, to believe that it was just the Earl of Warwick whose supporters felt the need to inscribe their symbol into the walls of the parish church? Probably not.

As long ago as 1967, Violet Pritchard noted that the ragged staff was far too common a motif recorded in church graffiti to only be associated with the earls of Warwick. It turned up just too often, when other badges made no appearance at all, and was commonly found associated with other symbols that had a recognised religious or devotional function. Pritchard suggested that this was probably also the case with the ragged staff – rather than being just a feudal livery badge the ragged staff was actually a religious symbol. Pritchard's conclusion is perhaps supported by the fact that a number of the medieval lead livery badges that are now in museum collections across the country also tend to include religious imagery in their decoration – such as crosses and Latin phrases – suggesting that their interpretation as purely heraldic badges may well be a mistake. Given that religious imagery from the Middle

Ages is full of ragged-staff symbols in one form or another, from the most common depictions of St Christopher with his staff, to the far less common depictions of the 'Tree of Jesse' (essentially a family tree of the bloodline of Christ, and a shorthand notation for Christ himself), it appears likely that the symbolism is far more complex than that associated solely with the livery of one noble family.

St Christopher was a key saint in the iconography of the medieval church, as shown by the surprisingly large number of medieval wall paintings of the saint still found today in parish churches such as Slapton in Northamptonshire. The image was traditionally located on the wall opposite the south door of the church, with the idea that anyone viewing the image of the saint through the open church door would be safe from sudden and unexpected death for that day, and safe on any journeys that they were planning to undertake. While there are a few problems with this traditional interpretation – particularly the number of written records that clearly show that most churches were locked between service times – St Christopher was clearly an important and well-loved saint among medieval churchgoers. As a number of ragged-staff graffiti inscriptions have been recorded around areas where images of St Christopher were probably once painted, such as those located around the north door of St Peter Hungate church in Norwich, it is quite possible that many of these inscriptions relate to a devotional cult surrounding the saint rather than any particular attachment to the earls of Warwick. Similarly, the fact that a number of the lead-cast livery badges are decorated with references to the Virgin Mary may suggest that even that interpretation is too simplistic, and that the livery badges, graffiti and second-hand symbolism is, once again, telling us only a fragment of a far larger, and largely lost, story. That the ragged staff has a religious dimension appears unquestionable, although the exact nature of that symbolism, for the time being, remains unknown. It had meaning – but we just don't yet know quite what it was.

The same that can be said about the ragged-staff symbol can also be applied to quite a number of other symbols that are sometimes taken to be heraldic. These include the fleur-de-lis, which is a fairly common graffiti inscription. Although obviously used in heraldry, including the medieval coat of arms of the kings of England and France, the fleur-de-lis was deeply associated with the cult of the Virgin Mary, and became synonymous with the Virgin herself. It can be regarded as 'her' flower, and is a standard feature in virtually all depictions of the Annunciation. It is therefore quite likely that a collection of fleurs-de-lis inscribed into the stone pillars near a Lady chapel or Mary altar are religious or devotional in nature rather than having anything to do with heraldry.

Perhaps one of the most intriguing aspects concerning heraldic graffiti is that of all the medieval-graffiti inscriptions that you are likely to come across, it is among the most likely to have been deliberately damaged or defaced. Accidental and wholesale destruction has most certainly taken place in the past, particularly during renovations and restorations, but, in very general terms, deliberate damage to early graffiti inscriptions is really rather rare. In recent centuries, the inscriptions have usually been rather difficult to see, unless very deeply cut into the stonework, or covered in layer upon layer of limewash, which has led to them being largely overlooked by both scholars and anyone intent on their destruction. However, graffiti inscriptions that were clearly visible for several centuries before the whitewash of the Reformation hid them from view have also tended to escape any subsequent 'vandalism'. This might purely be that as the vast majority of these early graffiti inscriptions were devotional in nature, or had a spiritual aspect, it was considered inappropriate to destroy them. The destruction of a prayer might well bring down some unlooked-for vengeance from above, or the defacing of an appeal to the saints could well incur their wrath. As such, many of these inscriptions remained untouched, and even respected, for many hundreds of years.

The same cannot, sadly, be said of heraldic inscriptions. This seemingly deliberate bias against these inscriptions can be seen at numerous churches across England. At Bale in north Norfolk, well known for its fantastic surviving medieval glass and painted consecration crosses, the door frame to the stair that once led to the rood loft has a number of small graffiti inscriptions, among which are what appear to be crude merchant's marks and what were once a number of heraldic shields. Although one or two of the shield designs are still clear enough to pick out elements of the heraldry, including a 'bend sinister', all of the shields have been badly damaged and aggressively defaced. The shields have been hacked away at and deeply gouged out, leaving shallow shield-shaped depressions in the stonework, while the markings around them remain largely untouched. Similar patterns can be seen elsewhere, such as further east at Swannington, where another shield carved around the main doorway has suffered deep gouges across its surface.

One possible reason for these deliberate attacks on heraldic graffiti may well be the subject matter itself. While many other inscriptions have a devotional and religious aspect, these inscriptions are only normally associated with individuals and families. Where the damaging of a votive inscription may be considered to bring down the wrath of God upon you, the destruction of something associated only with a noble or his family is unlikely to have the same result – unless the destroyer is perhaps caught in the act. In fact, the destruction of an individual's coat of arms in this way may have been regarded as a pretty effective way of insulting the individual involved. Indeed, it may well be that such directed and deliberate destruction actually had a far more sinister intention than that of a simple insult.

This perhaps leads us back to considering who actually created these heraldic inscriptions in the first place. While it was recorded by the likes of William Wey that many of these inscriptions were created by the knights and nobles themselves, as a memento of their visit, does this include all those now found in English parish churches? It would appear unlikely. In the first place, as we have seen, many of these heraldic inscriptions are clearly not accurate depictions of coats of arms, but rather generic depictions of stylised shields – which are unlikely to have been the result of absent-mindedness on the part of the visiting knight or nobleman. Secondly, while the creation of such a memento might well be expected of a nobleman undertaking the journey of a lifetime to one of the most sacred sites in Christendom, is it to be expected during a visit to a local parish church? In addition, if this was the case, then surely we would see far greater numbers of heraldic graffiti concentrated at popular English shrine sites such as Canterbury, Walsingham, Salisbury and Durham – which we simply don't find. Perhaps, then, it is worth considering another option? Here, we have heraldic graffiti, most likely *not* created by the owners of the coats of arms themselves, being deliberately damaged and defaced. While these may have been inscriptions created by one individual and then damaged by another, it is also worth considering that the person who created the graffiti may well have been the same individual who then, quite deliberately, destroyed it. Like the medieval curses from Norwich Cathedral, and the Roman curses of a thousand years earlier, perhaps these scratched-out heraldic inscriptions represent a deliberate cycle of creation and ritual destruction, a ritual act where the name of the individual is replaced by a symbol that is no less personal and unique; intentional acts of defacement designed to bring down ill-will upon the subject of the 'curse' – in this case, the owners of the coats of arms.

As with most types of medieval graffiti, it is most likely that there is more than one explanation and more than one thing going on. Some of the examples that have been recorded, at sites such as Worlington and Carlisle Castle, are undoubtedly meant to represent real coats of arms and, therefore, real people. These particular inscriptions may well have been created by those individuals as a memento of their visit. Other examples, such as that recovered from Bermondsey Abbey, may well have been aspirational in nature; perhaps making them a prayer (or a wish at the very least) that the creator of the inscription would one day be able to boast a coat of arms of their own. Others, perhaps, have less wholesome connotations, acting as marks to identify those upon whom bad luck and ill chance were to be drawn down. Whatever the case, these heraldic inscriptions litter the walls of our medieval churches and chapels. Many centuries later, the dust that is all that remains of once-great noble families now lies mingled with that of their servants and commoners, blown across the stone-flagged floors of draughty churches. Their coats of arms, still cut deep into the walls, leave them nameless and anonymous; empty and soundless fragments of a passed age.

CHAPTER THIRTEEN

MASON'S MARKS

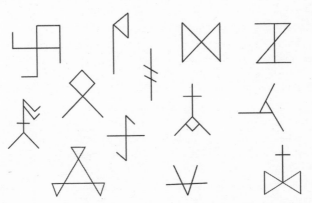

A small selection of 'mason's marks' recorded in English churches

'The master masons, holding measuring rod and gloves in their hands, say to others: "cut here", and they do not work; nevertheless they receive the greater fees'

Attributed to Nicolas de Biard, C13th

O f all the inscribed marks you are likely to come across in medieval churches, abbeys and cathedrals, the very oldest are likely to be those that were put there by the masons, those individuals actually involved in the construction of these superb buildings. These mason's marks are sometimes quite difficult to spot, often being placed high up on arches or other out-of-the-way places. Also sometimes known today as 'bankers' marks (after the stone bench or 'banker' upon which masons traditionally worked), these symbols are quite distinctive and separate from the more common graffiti. In general, a mason's mark tends to be well cut and neatly executed and, when compared to much of the traditional graffiti, clearly gives the impression of being the work of a professional. The marks themselves are usually made up of a series of straight-cut lines, meaning that they tend to be an angular assortment of stars, pentangles, diamonds and triangles; medieval mason's marks only very rarely include curves. It has also been pointed out that there appear to be lots of similarities between these marks and early Anglo-Saxon or Scandinavian runes. However, although both are made from straight lines, no direct link can be proved and there do not appear to be any direct crossovers. In fact, some of the earliest recognised marks take the form of a triangle with another single line attached to one of the points, and is meant to represent the mason's 'axe' – the tool used to shape the stones themselves. Every mason would possess such an axe and it was soon regarded as the symbol most generally associated with all masons, in much the same way that a horseshoe and hammer became associated with blacksmiths.

The mason's marks themselves have long been recognised and have been the subject of many academic studies, most usually trying to understand exactly what these simple markings can tell us about a building's construction history. It is generally believed that mason's marks were applied to finished stones as a simple form of quality control, and to enable the master mason or building financier to calculate the payments due to individual masons working on the project. On larger projects, medieval masons would work in gangs or groups, under the control and watchful eye of the master mason, who also doubled as the project's architect. Each mason would only be paid according to the amount of work he had completed, hence the need for accurate recording of exactly who had done what. In addition to this accountancy role, mason's marks must also have acted as a form of maker's mark – a simple 'I made this' symbol applied to the stones – in the same way that medieval blade-smiths, armourers and carpenters would also mark their work. How else can one explain churches where entire building phases have only a single mason's mark inscribed into them numerous times? With only one mason working on a site, the idea of these marks having any accounting function would perhaps be a little fanciful.

Mason's marks have also been used to try to identify individual medieval masons and, by doing so, identify other buildings that they may have worked on; and many such studies have taken place in recent decades – not all with a great deal of success. One of the problems surrounding the investigation of medieval architecture, and particularly its development, is that very few records survive relating to the masons who actually constructed these magnificent buildings. True, there are a number of surviving accounts and contracts relating to the construction of major monasteries and cathedrals that actually name the master mason, such as that relating to Beverley Minster, but these are extreme rarities. While local church accounts and churchwarden's records may mention a building alteration or rebuilding, these accounts are almost always related solely to the costs involved, and the individuals actually doing the work barely rate a mention. Only in a few very specific cases, such as the Suffolk village of Walberswick, do the accounts actually mention the name of the man employed. Here the building's accounts for 1426 make mention of a Richard Russell, who is to be employed to rebuild the church tower, although, even in this case, it is known that Russell was not working alone. Intriguingly, there is a carved stone that survives from the tower that appears to contain the initials 'R R', which, it has been suggested, was Russell's own commemoration of his work there.

However, cases such as Walberswick really are quite rare. As a result, historians and archaeologists have been left identifying the work of individual master masons based purely upon the stylistic similarities of different churches. While the work of certain unnamed individuals such as the 'Wiveton Master', named after the church on the north Norfolk coast where his work was first noted, can clearly be seen at a number of other local sites from the same period it is rarely that clear-cut. Some of the few medieval manuscripts to survive that relate to masons' design work suggest that the masons were certainly not above copying the style of their competitors, so it is easy to understand why academics would latch onto the idea of mason's marks as a quick and relatively easy way of establishing who did what and when. Sadly, it is rather rare that anything to do with medieval architecture is so easily explained. In the first place, not all medieval churches appear to contain mason's marks. Many examples, we must assume, may have been lost through erosion and rebuilding over the centuries, but there are a very large number of buildings that appear to contain none at all. Why this should be so remains something of a mystery. At the other end of the spectrum, larger buildings, such as St Albans Abbey, York Minster, Carlisle Cathedral or Norwich Cathedral, may contain dozens of different mason's marks covering a huge time period. Cathedrals in particular are, contrary to popular belief, always being rebuilt and remodelled; for example, Norwich has seen major building works taking place in almost every century since it was first constructed. Sometimes this new work was the result of changing architectural styles and the whims of bishops, at other times it was the result of disasters such as major fires or building collapse. In some areas of Norwich Cathedral, there has been so much rebuilding and renovation work taking place century after century that the walls are a giant jigsaw puzzle of different stonework. The result is that you can find mason's marks dating back to the twelfth century sitting alongside those from the fifteenth century and, within a few metres of those, from the nineteenth century. In some cases, the mass of mason's marks found in various parts of a large building are one of the best indicators as to which parts of the structure belong to which building period, adding a great deal to the hidden history of some of our best-known and best-loved buildings.

Our smaller country churches tend to tell a different story. In most of them, having been subject to only two or three building phases, there are far fewer mason's marks – if any at all. Churches like All Saints, Litcham, in Norfolk, which was largely rebuilt in 1412 (and reconsecrated on St Botolph's Day of that year) contain the marks of only three different masons, all of whom appear to have worked on the north arcade. Neighbouring churches at Mileham and Beeston, although having building works undertaken at about the same time, appear to contain none. However, a dozen or so miles to the north, at Wighton in north Norfolk, the massive rebuilding programme that took place only a few years after that at Litcham has left the church covered in a mass of mason's marks. Wighton church is a very different building from Litcham. Built upon the scale of a small cathedral, the workmanship here is of the very best quality and would have required a highly skilled workforce. Historian and journalist Nick Trend has studied the building in detail and has identified at least fourteen different masons from their marks scattered about the building. Perhaps more interestingly, he has noted that it appears that one group of masons' marks were largely confined to the north side of the church, with a second group found mainly on the south side, suggesting that the masons at the time were working within set groups, or gangs. Nick Trend went on to look at a number of surrounding churches of similar date, and there he found many of the same masons' marks, indicating that the masons involved in the building of Wighton were also responsible for work at East Winch, Little Walsingham, Weasenham St Peter, St Martin's at Fincham – and even Litcham. Some of those same masons were also identified as having worked on St Nicholas's chapel in King's Lynn, which is widely considered to be one of the finest churches of its time anywhere in the county.

While studies such as those carried out by Nick Trend – confined as it was to a limited area and a relatively short time period – can start to highlight more about the way in which medieval masons operated, and how their whole trade may have been structured, we should be cautious when looking at mason's marks as a whole. As other specialists have noted, there are only so many easy and angular designs that can be created with a mason's chisel and a few straight lines; as a result, certain mason's marks tend to get re-used. While it was once suggested that mason's marks, like coats of arms, were passed from father to son, there doesn't appear to be very clear evidence to support this idea. Far more likely is that masons operating in different parts of the country, and sometimes centuries apart, simply adopted very similar simple markings. Just as confusingly, it appears that individual masons may actually have altered or changed their own marks. When working in larger groups, at sites such as Wighton, masons with too-similar marks appeared to have adopted new ones, sometimes perhaps only for the duration of a particular contract. The result is that the evidence of mason's marks, while still fascinating, may be a little more complex than at first imagined. Those simple marks, cut into the stone as a symbol of a craftsman's pride in a job well done, still have the potential to tell us a very great deal about a trade that is still shrouded in mysteries and craft secrets. They may not be able to provide us with all the answers, but they are signposts to a better understanding. An understanding not just of these great buildings, but of those individuals who, many centuries ago, took rough and raw stone quarried from the earth and created masterpieces that soared towards the heavens.

One of the many fish inscriptions discovered in English churches, St Mary's church, Troston, Suffolk

Bird inscriptions are common discoveries in English parish churches, such as this example from St Mary's church, Parham, Suffolk

Beautifully executed inscription of a horse, St Michael and All Angel's church, Barton Turf, Norfolk.

An elaborate and possibly allegorical bird and tree inscription, St Andrew's church, Field Dalling, Norfolk

A rare example of medieval musical notation, Norwich Cathedral, Norfolk

Medieval harp inscription, St Mary's church, Parham, Suffolk

One of only two representations of medieval organs so far discovered, St Mary's church, Parham, Suffolk

Medieval text inscription that translates as 'John Lydgate made this with licence on the feast of Saints Simon and Jude'. St Mary's church, Lidgate, Suffolk

Unfinished medieval text inscription in the style of an illuminated capital, St Nicholas' church, Blakeney, Norfolk

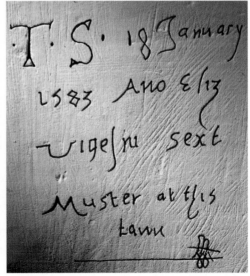

A brief account of a late sixteenth century military muster, St Mary's church, Lidgate, Suffolk

The VV symbol; one of the most common ritual protection marks found in English churches, St Mary's church, Mary in the marsh, Kent

One of the very few runic inscriptions discovered in England, which reads 'Tolfink wrote these runes on this stone', Carlisle Cathedral, Cumbria

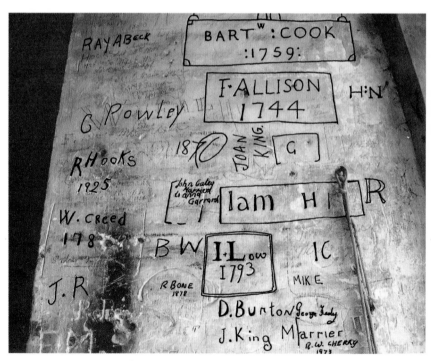

The inside of the ringing chamber in the tower of All Saint's church, Litcham, Norfolk

Medieval Latin inscription recording the arrival of the plague in the mid-fourteenth century, St Mary's church, Ashwell, Hertfordshire

Medieval Latin inscription, which reads Miserie mei deus ('May God have mercy upon me'), St Mary's church, Sawston, Cambridgeshire

Early Norman font decorated with compass-drawn designs, All Saint's church, Toftrees, Norfolk

Elaborate late medieval graffiti showing the martyrdom of St Edmund, Carlisle castle, Cumbria

Deeply carved depiction of St Katherine in the medieval chapel, Norwich castle, Norfolk

An example of a Mass Dial, or early sundial, St Margaret's church, Worthing, Norfolk

The monumental west front of Binham Priory, which is the site of the earliest known use of Gothic 'Bar' tracery in England, Binham Priory, Binham, Norfolk

CHAPTER FOURTEEN

MEN OF WEALTH AND POWER: MERCHANT'S MARKS

Typical medieval merchant's mark, Troston, Suffolk

'Might I but know thee by thy Household badge . . .'

William Shakespeare, Henry VI, *Part 2*

A merchant's mark was a small symbol used by a merchant or trader in place of a signature. They are, in effect, early trademarks and not unlike the idea of a commercial logo today. They were used in a wide variety of ways, from marking a merchant's goods and signing documents to being carved on their house or personal possessions. Although called 'merchant's marks', they were not just confined to the use of traders and, for those below the level of nobility, appear to have been used in much the same way as a coat of arms was used by the upper classes. As a result, we see these marks carved into the tombs of the prosperous lower orders and even appearing on brass memorial tablets. According to F.A. Girling, who studied the subject back in the middle of the twentieth century, these marks could also be handed down from one generation to the next, just like a coat of arms, with perhaps only minor differences or amendments between generations. Girling also makes note of the case of Susan Parker of Ipswich. After the death of her husband, Augustine, in the late sixteenth century, Susan continued in business alone into the early years of the seventeenth century. Rather than creating her own merchant's mark, she simply adopted the mark of her dead husband, differencing it slightly with the addition of the letter 'S'.

Merchant's marks are common finds in our medieval churches and cathedrals, and are often to be found clustered together in areas of the church. Although often mistaken for mason's marks, these symbols are usually very distinctly different. Where mason's marks tend to be made up of just straight lines, and are clearly created by a skilled individual, merchant's marks tend to be more fluid and less well made. In addition, where mason's marks are usually rather simple-looking, merchant's marks can be a complex motif involving symbols and lettering – more complex ones appearing as complete monograms. Many of them include very recognisable forms, such as the letters 'M' or 'V', or the arabic numeral '4'.

The earliest recorded merchant's marks appear to go back at least as far as the middle of the thirteenth century and, unsurprisingly, are to be found in the records of the great medieval trade centres of Norwich, London and Bristol. Given that tradesmen have been marking their goods long before that, and that these marks appear to be an extension of that practice, it is likely that there were many earlier examples that have been lost. Although they, like the mason's marks, can upon occasion rather look like the runic inscriptions of the Anglo-Saxon period, there doesn't appear to be any direct link between the two. In fact, many of the earlier merchant's marks look rather less like runic inscriptions than some of the later ones. However, the practice has obviously been going on a very long time.

In medieval churches, merchant's marks turn up quite frequently and many of these appear to have been placed there as part of the more formal decoration. In some cases, such as stained-glass examples, they may be there to record the individual who paid for its creation. The marks are also to be found on items such as monumental brasses and tombs, a form of decoration that would, had the individual been of higher social status, undoubtedly, have been replaced by a heraldic inscription. However, the vast majority of the merchant's marks that are recorded tend to be the more informal graffiti inscriptions. In some cases, such as Blakeney church in Norfolk, these marks are found inscribed together in small concentrations on one particular pillar of the church; a pattern that has also been noted in larger buildings, such as Norwich Cathedral. Perhaps, in these cases, the marks are clustered around areas of the church that had particular significance, either spiritually or for the merchants involved. In other cases, such as at St Nicholas's chapel in King's Lynn and Lidgate church in Suffolk, single examples are to be found etched into the door surrounds or porch. A particularly interesting collection of these marks is to be found at Wiveton church on the north Norfolk coast. Here, the same mark, very deeply cut into the stonework, appears on pillars of the north arcade. All are at about eye level and are so deeply inscribed as to suggest that they are far more than the usual graffiti inscription. As they only appear on this side of the church, and are clearly visible even without specialist lighting, it has been suggested that they may be territorial in nature; linked perhaps to an individual who perhaps paid for the rebuilding of the arcade itself.

The most useful aspect of a merchant or individual using a mark rather than a written signature is that it has the advantage of being understandable to both the literate and illiterate. In a medieval society where a good proportion of people could do little more than read and write their own name, the advantages are obvious. Although modern historians now believe that a far larger number of people in the later Middle Ages had basic literacy skills than was once thought, their level of schooling was, at best, limited. A simple monogram might spell out letters to those who could read but, even to those few who were completely unlettered, it would still have been a recognisable symbol. They didn't need to be able to read the letters – just be able to recognise the pattern they made. In this way, marks certainly functioned like a modern business logo or trademark, with people able to identify a commercial organisation just from a symbol, many of which are still far from dissimilar from their medieval counterparts.

Until very recently, it was believed that all these symbols were most probably related to individual merchants or tradespeople. Each mark may, perhaps, have been passed down a generation or two, with minor changes and differences, but they still related to an individual, family or merchant dynasty. However, recent discoveries at a number of sites have meant that the traditional view is now open to question. To anybody visiting Carlisle Cathedral today, the most notable point of interest – which will undoubtedly be pointed out by one of the well-informed volunteer guides – is the runic inscription located near the south door. One of two such inscriptions in the building – the other being high up and not on public display – it is now safely protected behind a glass frame. However, if you take a short walk into the choir of the cathedral, you will soon come across some other inscriptions that are certainly just as interesting, and potentially just as significant. Here, carved into the woodwork of a very fine set of late-medieval stalls, complete with the most wonderful (and sometimes disturbing) misericords, can be seen one of the most extensive collections of merchant's marks anywhere in England. All of them appear to date to the very last years of the sixteenth century, a time when Carlisle was an important regional trade centre near to the English–Scottish border, and most of the marks date to either 1591 or 1597. What is extraordinary about them is that, although most of them are of slightly different dates, and all of them carry differing sets of initials, they all have the same, or almost identical, merchant's marks at the centre.

Although they certainly look like merchant's marks found elsewhere, it would appear that they are probably not. Merchant's marks were meant to be easily recognisable, allowing people to quickly identify the person they related to. The fact that these marks all look basically the same would suggest that these had another purpose entirely. This isn't just a problem that relates to Carlisle alone. In many other churches and cathedrals, what appears to be the same mark is repeated many times, either with or without initials, and the same marks can be seen in churches scattered across an area or region. The fact that so many of these marks were almost identical – therefore, rather defeating the object of a merchant's mark in the first place – was even noted by Girling back in the 1960s as something that he could not easily account for.

It is much more likely that these markings all relate to these individuals' membership of a common organisation, most likely a trade guild of some sort; and that the central symbol is, in fact, the mark of that specific guild. Such trade guilds were the social and economic backbone of most medieval and Tudor towns. They drew their members from specific traders, such as the glovers, merchants or butchers, and would have regulated the trade activities within the town, acted as a quality-control board and even regulated prices. In addition, these guilds also had a social role, settling disputes between members, helping those who became too sick to work and even assuring a decent turn-out in the event of a guild member's funeral. Before the Reformation, many of these organisations operated as supposedly religious guilds, supporting activities in their parish church and often contributing quite large sums of money to the maintenance of certain church altars or parish lights. However, these overtly religious guilds were swept away during the Edwardian Reformation in the middle decades of the sixteenth century. Some were dissolved, their goods either taken by the crown or illegally redistributed locally, while others simply changed their names and structure to continue much as they had done before.

Late-sixteenth-century Carlisle is known to have been home to eight major guilds – the merchants, butchers, skinners, shoemakers, tanners, tailors, smiths and weavers – all of whom met at the city's Guildhall, which still survives to this day. It would appear likely that this particular symbol, repeated across the choir stalls of the cathedral, was actually the symbol of one of these guilds – although we may never know precisely which one – and that the letters are the initials of individual members. What, then, is the significance of the two dates, 1591 and 1597? With respect to the 1591 date, which is the least common on the carvings, no specific link is known. The 1590s were not a happy time in England generally, with continuing foreign entanglements acting as a drain on manpower and a number of exceptionally bad harvests making famine a very real possibility on several occasions. However, we do know that 1597 was a particularly significant year for Carlisle and the surrounding area; a year that has gone down in history as one of the most dreadful on record for those living in the north-west.

Early in 1597, the first victims of plague were reported in the Richmond area of North Yorkshire, and, within a few weeks, this epidemic had exploded westwards along the dales, leaving in its wake a trail of bereavement and empty smallholdings. The casualties, even by plague standards, were astronomically high and the disease's spread was sudden and erratic. That autumn, the plague hit the towns of Kendal, Penrith and Carlisle almost simultaneously, with devastating results. In Penrith, over six hundred souls – nearly half the population – were dead in the matter of a few months, with bodies quickly buried in hastily dug graves, local authority at the point of collapse and houses lying empty. It was the same story in the city of Carlisle itself. Local records for the period are unsurprisingly incomplete, but suggest an epidemic that outstripped even the Black Death of the mid-fourteenth century in its speed and ferocity, leading some modern biologists to actually rule out bubonic plague as the culprit. Although nobody can as yet be entirely certain exactly what this disease was, with anthrax even being seriously considered at one point, it was certainly the most virulent disease to have ever hit Carlisle and, as autumn turned to winter, the city began to suffer.

The city authorities did their very utmost to halt the spread of the disease and limit its impact, but with varying degrees of success. The city all but sealed itself off from the outside world, ejecting vagrants and strangers from the gates and refusing entry to those who came from areas where the plague was already known to be. Infected households were placed under a strict quarantine and bodies were quickly removed from houses where all had perished, leaving city employees to cleanse the dwellings as best they could, to try to prevent further infection. Regular inspections of households were instituted, to try to identify those who might be suffering from the illness, and isolation hostels were established outside the city walls. The city also instituted a poor relief fund, to help those who simply couldn't help themselves, and made sure that medical treatment was free to those who could not afford to pay for it. The richer townsfolk were also called upon to support the city authorities in their efforts, and the city council made funds available from the city chest – but all, sadly, to little avail. Modern studies suggest that the incubation period of this particular disease, whatever it may have been, was relatively long, meaning that by the time the city had put measures in place to stop its spread it was already too late – their walls had been breached many weeks before. A census of the townspeople taken in late December, before the plague had really started to bite, shows that, of the 323 households in the city, 242 were reported as being infected, with 149 deaths already having taken place. As the winter dragged on the death toll grew.

There is no consensus on the exact number of deaths that took place in Carlisle during the last months of 1597. The city's population is believed to have been somewhere in the region of 1,300 souls, and a plaque in Penrith church, which states that 1,196 people died in Carlisle, is most certainly an overestimate. The real figures were undoubtedly lower, and some records suggest that recovery from the disease was not entirely unheard of, but it appears likely that the winter of 1597 saw the deaths of about forty per cent of the city's inhabitants, at the very least. Perhaps, then, this is the answer to the puzzle of the merchant's marks all bearing that date in Carlisle Cathedral? If these carvings are meant to represent individual members of one of the city guilds, then could it be that they relate to this period when death stalked the streets of the city? A time when the role of a guild – to support individual members in life and to ensure their respectful and honoured passing from the world – would just not have been possible; a time when bodies were quickly removed to hastily dug graves leaving no time for ceremony, no time for remembrance and no time for memorials. Are these, then, the memorials to those guild members who, in the dark and cold of the winter of 1597, were caught in the claws of a plague that was stripping their city to the bare bones? Their fellow guild members, shuttered in the dark cathedral and awaiting either death or salvation, carving their friends' initials into the oak of the choir stalls, to stand testament for ever more.

CHAPTER FIFTEEN

OF KNIGHTS
AND DRAGONS

The eroded remains of St George, early fifteenth century, Weybread, Suffolk

'Seynt George, oure ladyes knight
on whom all Englond hath believe,
Show us thy helpe to god almyght
And kepe oure kyng from all myscheve'

Anon. C15th

To begin with, it should be pointed out that, despite the title of this chapter, there will be very few dragons actually making an appearance. Although the medieval church may have been crammed with images of dragons and mythical beasts, they simply don't appear very often as graffiti inscriptions. Exactly why this should be the case is something of a mystery. At present, there are only a handful of examples of other mythical beasts carved in graffiti. The church of St Bartholomew at Churchdown in Gloucestershire has a rather fine figure of a mermaid inscribed near the doorway. Resplendent with her traditional comb and mirror, she preens among other inscriptions that include what appears to be a head of Christ and a spouting whale. At North Cerney, near Cirencester, there is an inscription that is supposed to represent the mythical manticore, a beast with a human head, the body of a lion and the tail of either a dragon or a scorpion. While such imagery was popular in the late-Saxon church, when dragons and other beasts were common decorative motifs on manuscripts and in sculpture, their popularity has not translated into the graffiti inscriptions. However, with the arrival of the Normans, it soon becomes apparent that dragon images, at least – particularly those associated with St George – continue to be a theme in our churches, with multiple examples sometimes to be found in the same church.

At the beautiful church of Swannington, you can still see no less than four superb images of medieval dragons. The most obvious is that to be found in one of the spandrels to the late-medieval porch, sitting opposite an image of St Catherine – the church's dedicatory saint. However, the real surprise awaits you inside. At the far end of the chancel, is a rather amazing survival from the years just after the Norman Conquest. Set into the corner is an elaborately carved bowl, or 'stoup', that would originally have contained holy water for people to cross themselves with as they entered the church. On three sides of the square bowl are the most stunningly detailed Norman carvings of St George and the dragon, with the image of St George looking as though it had just walked off the Bayeux Tapestry. The fourth side is uncarved, suggesting it was originally intended to sit against a wall. Perhaps just as remarkable as the carving itself is the story of the stoup's survival. Most such holy-water stoups, unless physically set into the walls of the church, were destroyed at the Reformation, and this example, with its obviously traditional decoration, would have been a prime target for the reformers and Puritans who came after them. However, the stoup was obviously valued by the local congregation. When the time came to remove such objects from the church, along with the rood screen and images of the saints, the parish hid the stoup in the old stairway to the now-defunct rood loft and bricked it up, leaving it to be safely redis-covered many centuries later.

Such an early depiction of St George and the dragon is really quite unusual. Although today considered to be England's patron saint, the real popularity of St George didn't begin until quite late in the Middle Ages. Prior to St George, England cannot really be considered to have had a single patron saint. However, there were three saints who appeared time and time again, often together, and were certainly asso-ciated with the English monarchy: St Edmund, St Edward the Confessor and St John the Baptist. These royal saints, however, had one major drawback as far as the later Plantagenet kings of England were concerned – they just weren't military enough. The most high-profile advancement of St George came with the establishment of the chivalric Order of the Garter by Edward III, who directly associated the saint with all the most highly prized qualities of knighthood. This initial promotion of the cult was soon followed by more general popularity among those involved with the military. At the height of the decades-long war with France, both Henry IV and Henry V began to promote the cult of St George as a more martial saint upon which Englishmen could call in times of need. Taking their lead from the top, the people of England also began to look to St George as their 'special' saint and, throughout the fifteenth century, the cult grew with vigour. It is from this period that we begin to find records reflecting the growth of the cult, with donations and bequests for images and paintings of St George making regular appear-ances in the wills of the time. According to the records, at one time, there were at least one hundred wall paintings to St George in our parish churches, although fewer than fifty now survive in even fragmentary form; among the finest are those at Hardham in West Sussex, Troston, and at Hornton, Oxfordshire.

Given this growth and popularity of the cult, it is perhaps even more surprising that we find so few depictions of St George and the dragon in the graffiti inscriptions of our churches. To date, there have only been four possible discoveries of dragons, both with and without St George figures, and at least one of these discoveries is slightly suspect. A brief and sketchy outline of what appears to be St George and the dragon can be found in Eastwood church in Essex, while a singular dragon appears at Crowhurst in Surrey, with another recently discovered example being found at Finchingfield in Essex. At Marsham in Norfolk, a splendid little tableaux is to be found carved into one of the pier bases that appears to show St George doing battle against a strange upright-looking dragon. However, the fact that the dragon appears to have a fringe running along its base has led to the suggestion that it may well be a representation of actors – or mummers, as they were known – in costume, performing a medieval entertainment or play. The finest depiction of St George and the dragon is perhaps to be found at Weybread in Suffolk. Although badly weathered and now incomplete, the original inscription was created by a talented individual with an eye for detail. What remains today is a figure of the upper half of a knight in detailed early-fifteenth-century armour. Part of a saddle can be shown rising up behind his waist, indicating that he was originally shown mounted, and both arms are raised up to thrust his lance downwards towards a few sketchy lines that are all that remain of the dragon's head. The depiction is so similar in style to a number of surviving medieval wall paintings and manuscript illustrations that it is hard to think it was not inspired by just such a depiction that was once to be found in the church.

While images of dragons may be in short supply among the graffiti found in our churches, images of knights and armed men most certainly aren't. Given that the period of the Hundred Years War was followed almost immediately by the sporadic conflict known today as the Wars of the Roses, barely a decade passed in the fourteenth and fifteenth centuries without English soldiers being involved in some form of military action. Many of these were bloody battles fought on the other side of the Channel, but the low-level conflict from 1450 onwards brought strife very much into the English countryside and the English parish. The Wars of the Roses may be viewed by some as a series of short campaigns and battles interspersed by times of relative peace, but one need only read detailed contemporary accounts, such as the letters of the Paston family, to realise that even these relatively tranquil moments could be blighted by violence. With ungoverned and unemployed soldiers often to be found among the ranks of the itinerant wanderers of the countryside, it is hardly a surprise that images of armed men and knights are to be found in large quantities among the graffiti.

The images of armed men are to be found all over the country and vary greatly in the quality of their depiction. Some, such as the miniature battle or hunting scene from Shoreham-by-Sea in West Sussex, are shown as faint outlines of figures armed with what appear to be a mix of longbows, crossbows and polearms. At Chalgrave in Bedfordshire, the armed figures are most probably meant to depict knights with sword and shield, but are little more than stylised and inflated stick figures, making it difficult to draw too many conclusions as to what they were originally meant to show. However, at Leighton Buzzard and Shillington, also in Bedfordshire, are two extremely neatly made images that can tell us a great deal about both what they show and when they were made. At Shillington, the single head of a knight is shown in full profile, wearing a helmet and mail aventail, or hood. There are also lines shown that suggest they represent the cords that actually attached the aventail to the helmet, typically seen on high-quality armour in the late fourteenth or early fifteenth century. In contrast, the single figure from Leighton Buzzard appears to entirely lack a head, worn away with the passing of the years. Here is shown a full-length figure standing with one hand holding a polearm or halberd and the other tucked into his belt, the attitude of a figure standing guard that can be seen in numerous manuscript illustrations. He is also shown wearing a short, highly pleated gown or doublet, with thick padded shoulders and a raised collar, absolutely typical of fashionable menswear in the second half of the fifteenth century. A very similar figure, but this time armed with two swords, is to be found at Horseheath in Cambridgeshire, while another, armed only with a long dagger, is to be found on the door surround at Woolpit church in Suffolk. At Croxton Kerrial in Leicestershire can be seen an almost identically dressed figure, again in tightly pleated short gown and with a short, slightly conical hat upon his head. This time, however, the figure is clearly armed with a tapering thrusting sword and a small circular shield known as a buckler. Such shields were popular in the late fifteenth century, and are often quoted as the source of the term 'swashbuckler', derived from the noisy fighting style of sword blades clanging on the metal of the shield. Another use of the buckler is to be found on the image of a fully armoured knight from Goxhill in Lincolnshire, again dated to the fifteenth century, who stands with sword and shield outstretched as if for battle. Although highly stylised, it is clear that the Goxhill figure was meant to represent a man-at-arms, or knight.

Alongside the depictions of knights and men-at-arms are occasionally discovered images of the lower orders at war, most notably the archers. A mad-looking archer, with hair sprouting from the top of his head like a small fountain, can be seen at Thurlow Magna church in Suffolk, while a small group of apparently battling archers are clustered around the base of the tower arch at Great Witchingham in Norfolk. At Chalgrave in Bedfordshire, archers are to be found among the other fighting figures that dance across the stonework, and at Whittlesford, Cambridgeshire, a single archer is to be found on the western tower arch. Such depictions, though, are actually quite rare when compared to the numbers of inscriptions that show armed men, which might be considered rather strange given just how common longbows were in everyday life at the time. The regulation of the longbow and its use derived from the Statute of Winchester, which dated back to the late thirteenth century, and which in turn was derived from the Assize of Arms of 1181. The law laid down precisely the responsibilities for all levels of society to aid in their country's defence, including what equipment each man was to provide and how local defence was to be organised. For example, the Assize of Arms stated that a knight was to provide himself with a 'coat of mail, shield and lance', with poorer freemen required only to supply 'a lance and iron helmet'. The Assize of Arms was expanded upon by the Statute of Winchester in 1285, stating that 'all others who can do so shall have bows and arrows outside the forests'. To be found carrying a bow within the king's forest, led to a presumption of poaching – and the harsh penalties that that entailed. What the Statute did was guarantee that, at any one time, the king could potentially call upon tens of thousands of trained archers, and the longbow would have been one of the commonest items in medieval society. To give an indication of the numbers of bows actually available, you need only look at the lists of stores kept in the Tower of London, one of the Crown's main arsenals. As late as 1547, when the longbow was busily being replaced with the new-fangled handguns, there were still over three thousand bows in store, with several thousand more scattered around the smaller fortifications controlled by the Crown. In every village in England could be found dozens of longbows and hundreds of arrows – and yet their popularity simply isn't reflected in the graffiti.

Alongside the figures of armed men, it is not uncommon to come across examples of just the weapons themselves. Leaving aside depictions of shields, and their possible heraldic associations, you can come across axes, as at Bletchingley in Surrey, swords and daggers, as at Keddington in Suffolk and Sawston in Cambridgeshire, arrows, as at Oxted in Surrey and Trunch in Norfolk, or collections of every sort of medieval weapon you can think of, as at Swannington. The Swannington graffiti are really quite extraordinary. Located very near the ground, they are etched very, very lightly into one of the massive pillars that support the tower and are extremely difficult to see. However, upon closer inspection, you will be able to make out an entire armoury for a medieval fighting man. A sword lies alongside a large shield, with a longbow and an arrow carved just below them. To the far side are a number of what were probably originally meant to be poleaxes, now quite worn, and a very clear depiction of a glaive or military billhook. Exactly why there are just so many weapons clustered together at Swannington, or exactly why they were created almost at floor level, remains unexplained.

Of course, it isn't difficult to come up with many, many reasons as to why armed men and their weapons should feature quite so prominently among the medieval-graffiti inscriptions. It is, however, far harder to suggest just which of those explanations might be the most likely. Most certainly, the image and idea of the medieval knight was something that people aspired to. We need only look at the literature of the age to understand just how deeply embedded in society was the concept of the chivalric knight. It is also worth remembering that one of the first, and most popular, books to have come off William Caxton's early printing press was the epic retelling of the legends of King Arthur – Sir

Thomas Malory's *Le Morte d'Arthur* – which was soon followed by a number of other popular chivalric romances. While not everyone in society ever had a chance of actually aspiring to the level of knighthood, the concepts associated with them, and the chivalric deeds of legend, were most certainly popular at all levels. It is, of course, possible that many of these inscriptions are in no way related to reality anyway. With the popularity of such tales as King Arthur, it may well be that the images merely reflect that popularity, showing images that their creators associated with the tales rather than real life. There was no aspiration involved, just a reflection of what interested and entertained.

There is one major counter-argument to those ideas, and it is a simple one. While knights are most certainly a popular theme among the graffiti, so too are archers, weapons and armed men, who, even with the best will in the world, it is impossible to think of as being directly associated with knighthood. They are shown with the weapons of the common man, used by the foot soldiers of the armies that had marched their way across the fields of both England and France. Although the sword, shield and lance of the knights are present, so too are the bows, arrows, billhooks and glaives of the lower orders. They talk of warfare and butchery rather than knightly tournament and chivalry. These, then, perhaps reflect something deeper going on upon the walls of our churches, an echo of the chaos that English society found itself in for much of the fifteenth century. While reading the romances of the chivalric knights, and building more magnificent monuments to the glory of God, they are a stark reminder of the anarchy and bloodshed that could all too easily overtake even the quietest community.

There is of course one group of knights who, wherever you visit, do appear to receive the blame for a very great deal of medieval graffiti – the Knights Templar. This order of monastic warriors was first formed to protect the lives and interests of poor pilgrims travelling to and from the Holy Land. However, the order soon outgrew its humble origins and became one of the most powerful and influential cross-border organisations in medieval Europe. Their wealth outstripped that of most monarchs, and their direct allegiance to the pope made them exempt from national legislation and control. The Templars have been credited with developing one of the first international banking systems, and their financial influence made them a political force to be reckoned with. This, it has been argued, was their undoing. No monarch could stand by and allow an outside organisation to be seen as more powerful than himself, and no pope could allow the existence of a military order that thought it could directly influence the papacy. In 1307, the French-born Pope, Clement V, and King Philip of France conspired to bring down the whole order and end their dominance; this the pair achieved with remarkably little opposition, the order being officially disbanded in 1312. The order's possessions that had not already been sequestrated by various monarchs across Europe were handed to the Knights Hospitaller, and the Knights Templar officially ceased to exist. The manner of their downfall, and the nature of many of the accusations against them, which included the story that they denied Christ and worshipped the image of a head, has led to a continuing web of mystery and conspiracy being woven around the order. Despite the fact that almost everything to do with the order was well documented at the time of their downfall, they have come to be seen as the guardians of a great secret or a great treasure that still fascinates conspiracy theorists to this day, and some maintain that the order continues to exist, in secret.

As a result of the Knights Templars' enigmatic and mysterious reputation, they have, over the last century, tended to be the first to be blamed when something odd or strange from the medieval period is discovered. If strange gravestones are found in an old monastery – it must be the Templars. If unusual manuscripts are found in an old archive – it must be the Templars. And if ancient markings are founds on church walls – then it must surely be the Templars. You can, indeed, begin to see a pattern emerging, and medieval-graffiti inscriptions that had gone unrecorded for centuries were prime candidates to be laid at the door of the Knights Templar. It is, therefore, no surprise that when, in the middle of the eighteenth century, a cave carved out of the natural chalk and covered in hundreds of strange and wonderful medieval carvings was discovered beneath the town of Royston in Hertfordshire, it was immediately suggested this was the work of the Knights Templar.

Royston Cave is a truly remarkable site. The cave itself is roughly circular, only about five metres across and formed in a general bell shape. When it was first rediscovered, it was found to be half-full of soil and debris, after the removal of which it was seen that the chalk walls of the cave were quite literally covered in high-relief carvings that were clearly of medieval origin. Alongside images of the saints were scenes of the crucifixion, knights holding swords, rows of tiny people and strange markings. Many of the images were clearly religious in nature, although the densely packed wall surfaces sometimes made it difficult to identify individual scenes. Sadly, since its discovery, the cave has also received a whole new layer of carvings, created by the many eighteenth- and nineteenth-century visitors to the site who also felt the need to leave their own marks. However, for the last century and a half, the origins of the cave and carvings have been speculated upon, and the supposed link to the Knights Templar has become well and truly embedded in local legend. Perhaps unfortunately, there is absolutely no evidence to support it. Although there is one possible carving, among the many hundreds present, that purports to show an undisputable Templar symbol – of two poor knights upon the same horse – it transpires that this area of the cave was once quite badly damaged, and the carving is a restoration of somewhat dubious integrity. It is also clear from the carvings themselves that, apart from the more modern tourist graffiti, most of them date to the fifteenth century, more than two centuries after the Knights Templar were forcibly disbanded. In addition, although the quantity of the carvings found in Royston Cave is unusual, the carvings themselves really aren't. In fact, they can now be described as being fairly typical of the period.

If you want to see good parallels to the carvings found in Royston Cave, then it isn't English churches that you need to visit, but English medieval castles, and in particular the chapels within those castles. In the great Norman keep of Norwich Castle, tucked away in one corner of the upper level, is a small chamber that used to house the medieval chapel. Here, too, the walls are deeply cut with low-relief carvings. Alongside the heraldic inscriptions, images of castle fortifications and strange cross-carrying birds are found images of the saints that bear an uncanny resemblance to those found in Royston Cave. Cut during the later Middle Ages into the hard stone of the walls, they appear to sit in a strange limbo between formal decoration and graffiti, and must have taken many hours to make. As Norwich Castle was used as both an administrative centre and a prison, it is unclear exactly when, and by whom, the carvings were made. Many miles further north, almost an entire country away, the same sort of low-relief decoration can also be seen in the great keep at Carlisle Castle. The Carlisle carvings were created not in the chapel itself but in the entrance passageway to it, leading to many people suggesting that the carvings were the work of prisoners. Whatever the truth of the matter, what is clear is that at sites like Norwich and Carlisle, inscriptions were created that would not be out of place in Royston Cave – and at the same period. It would, therefore, appear more than likely that the carvings in Royston Cave have a similar origin, and that the cave may once have served as either a prison or a chapel.

It would, in fact, be true to say that there has never been a single piece of graffiti recorded in England that can be positively linked to the Knights Templar. There are no secrets from a long-disbanded medieval military order scratched onto the walls of our churches. While this may come as a disappointment to the conspiracy theorists determined to uncover long-lost and arcane truths, it really shouldn't be. The walls of our churches are full of hidden messages. They do conceal great mysteries and many of them certainly haven't been seen for centuries. However, rather than being the mysteries of long-lost knights and crusaders bent on world domination, they are the everyday mysteries of medieval faith and belief. They are the mysteries of life, love, marriage and death in the medieval parish; the mysteries of people's dreams, hopes and fears. The ability to catch even a glimpse of such mysteries, and understanding the lives of those who have gone before us, should be treasure enough for anyone.

CHAPTER SIXTEEN

THE PASSING OF THE HOURS: MASS DIALS

Very unusual compass-drawn design, Bedingham, Norfolk

'There is a time for everything,
and a season for every activity under the heavens:
a time to be born and a time to die'

Ecclesiastes 3:1

The chances are that anyone who has visited even a handful of medieval churches anywhere in the country will have come across a Mass dial, or scratch dial, etched into the outside of at least one of them. Although not strictly speaking graffiti, these early sundials are often found alongside early inscriptions. They usually take the form of a compass-drawn circle, or sometimes a rectangle, with a series of straight lines radiating out from a central point – just like a sundial, but most usually carved into a vertical surface. The central point is often a hole into which a stick or nail was once inserted, and in some cases the rusted remains of this can still be made out. These dials are most often to be seen on the south side of the church, sometimes located on the porch, a nearby pillar, or the priest's door leading in to the chancel. Many examples are very deeply etched into the stonework, suggesting that the lines have been gone over time and time again, and can usually be seen without any need for specialist lighting. The fact that they are so deeply cut into the building and are so easy to spot has meant that they have long been the subject of interest and examination. Indeed, these days, they actually have an entire society dedicated to them.

The British Sundial Society was formed in 1989, with the express purpose of promoting the study of this long-overlooked and fascinating area of timekeeping. The society soon found that many of its members had a more than passing interest in Mass dials, and a specialist Mass-dial section was soon established and continues to thrive to the present day. The Mass-dial section of the society aims to record all examples of these inscriptions across the country and place them on a searchable register or database that will be available to the public. The society makes it clear that these dials are not the same as traditional sundials, which are designed to mark off the hours of the day as accurate timepieces. The Mass dials were always only meant to show the approximate times of individual church services, and the marking can vary rather a lot between individual examples. What is clear, though, is that these inscriptions are really very common, with some counties able to boast of several hundred examples already known about.

Just as with more general graffiti inscriptions, the dating of these Mass dials is particularly fraught with danger. Early scholars studying them suggested that the cruder the inscription was, the earlier it was likely to be – and even came up with a form of style guide to support their theory. In essence, if it was just a simple circle with a few straight lines radiating outwards then it was likely to be early. If it was more complex, and particularly if it included numerals, then it was likely to be later. The problems with such a very convenient system are pretty obvious, and relied totally on the idea that these designs had evolved and become more complex over time. While that may well be true of things such as church architecture, it certainly isn't something that can be generally applied to inscriptions carved into the church stonework. To complicate matters further, there are a number of very early sundials that can be securely dated as belonging to the late-Anglo-Saxon period, such as that still to be seen at Kirkdale in North Yorkshire, and these are by no means simplistic. Indeed, the only reason that it was possible to date the Kirkdale inscription at all was the fact that it included examples of text that were clearly early in date and details of who commissioned it. Similarly, a number of quite elaborate examples, such as that from Helhoughton in Norfolk, included text that indicated that they date from the eighteenth or nineteenth century, and were more like the traditional sundial than any Mass dial. The result is rather a confusing mess. If we accept the traditional way of dating these dials, then we must also accept that Anglo-Saxon dials were highly decorative and complex in design, and that they underwent a sudden decline in quality with the arrival of the Normans, only to make a long and slow evolutionary climb back towards complexity in the seventeenth or eighteenth century. Put like this, the theory just doesn't make a great deal of sense; and while it may well be convenient, it certainly is not backed up by the evidence.

And that is rather the problem with Mass dials. None of it really makes any sense. Just about all the accepted wisdom concerning these inscriptions, not just with regards to dating, rather fails to stand up to close scrutiny. The most obvious problem with them is the actual interpretation of what they are supposed to be: simple sundials designed to indicate the times of church services. On the surface, that might make sense, but then you begin to look a little deeper and a number of questions present themselves. Let's think about this for a moment. Put yourself in the place of a medieval yeoman farmer, out ploughing in the fields in readiness to sow the next crop, or a medieval alewife busy brewing vast batches of ale. Suddenly, you realise that while you have been so busy the day has slipped away from you. Surely, you think, it must nearly be time for Mass? So what do you do? Do you immediately down tools, hasten to the church door and check the Mass dial? I think not. Given that medieval church services were advertised by the ringing of the bells, in much the same way as happens with Sunday services in many modern parishes, most people would have had ample warning that Mass (or whichever service) was to begin shortly. In addition, churchwardens' records show that many churches actually had clocks built into the towers from at least the late Middle Ages. Although they mainly appear in the written record, due to the frequency with which they needed repairing, it is clear that for many parishes these would have made the need for any Mass dials rather redundant.

Perhaps, then, these dials were to give notice to the bell ringers, and indicate to them when they should begin to announce the service? Perhaps they were for the use of the parish priest, to indicate the service times, which would at least explain the presence of a few of them near chancel doors. However, the problems don't stop there. While most of these dials are to be found on the south side of parish churches, particularly around the porch and doorway, there are a significant number that are found on other sides of the church, including the north side. Obviously, a Mass dial located on the north side of a church is simply not going to work. It just can't fulfil the function for which it was supposedly created. The usual interpretation is that these dials were inscribed into stones that were originally on the south side and have since been re-used during a rebuilding of the church, only to find themselves on the shadowy north side. While this might be possible, the sheer number of misplaced examples would tend to make this particular interpretation at least very improbable. Even in churches such as Worthing in Norfolk, which is so small and modest as to have been completed in only one or two building phases, a Mass dial, inscribed into a large section of stone, has found its way into the masonry of the east end. If it *is* re-used material then it is difficult to suggest exactly where it originally came from – because it most probably wasn't Worthing church itself.

Worthing is interesting in the fact that it rather highlights one of the other fundamental problems with the current interpretation of Mass dials. The dial found at the eastern end of this remote and modest church is meant to have been relocated there from the south side. However, the south side of the church already has an additional two or three Mass dials, all now to be found around the south doorway and inside the modest porch. Once again, the traditional interpretation is that the Mass dials were already there when the decision was made to build the porch – and they eventually found themselves inside a building where, once again, they couldn't possibly function. In the case of Worthing, where the south door is of confident Norman work and the porch a late-medieval addition, this could of course be the case. However, there are quite a number of churches where the porch and doorway appear to have been built at the same time, and yet Mass dials are still to be found inside. Which rather brings us to the third question concerning the traditional interpretation of these intriguing carvings. At Worthing, and at many, many other sites, we have not one but many examples of Mass dials. Some sites can boast as many as five or six examples spread across the building, almost always all but identical in design. Look again inside the porch at Worthing and you will find two Mass dials, one above the other, on the left-hand side of the doorway. At St Botolph's church, Ratcliffe on the Wreake in Leicestershire, you have no less than five almost-identical Mass dials laid out along the lower edge of a window surround. Why should this be so? What exactly is the point of having more than one? Are they meant to indicate the time in London, Paris and Rome? I think not. Are they all the work of copycat artists, who simply emulate the first dial that was inscribed into the stonework? Once again, it is possible – but, if this is the case, then these copycats went to a great deal of trouble to achieve very little.

These problems with the interpretation of Mass dials provide a great many questions, but very few answers. If these enigmatic little inscriptions are not meant to function as some form of time keeper, then exactly what were they for? Whatever they were intended for was obviously pretty clear to people living all over the country and, given their numbers, must have been widespread. Even supposing that the majority of them may have been used as some form of sundial, the sheer number of examples that do not fit this pattern and form is startling.

CHAPTER SEVENTEEN

BIRDS, FISH, PUFFINS AND PILGRIMS

Long-legged medieval bird, Leighton Buzzard, Bedfordshire

'Then folks long to go on pilgrimages
And palmers to seek strange shores
To far-off shrines, known in sundry lands'

Chaucer, The Canterbury Tales: The General Prologue

The problem with studying medieval-graffiti inscriptions is that, at the present time, there is simply so much that we don't know. There are just so many types of inscription that we come across time after time, in churches many hundreds of miles apart, that clearly had some meaning and significance at the time they were made and to the people that made them – but exactly what that significance was is now something of a mystery. We can make educated guesses based upon the evidence and context, certainly, but, without any additional evidence to support it, they remain working theories, a 'best guess', arrived at while stumbling around in the dark, and with the temptation as archaeologists to nod sagely and mumble the word 'ritual'. Perhaps even then, we are occasionally reading too much into some of these inscriptions. Maybe some of them are indeed just the doodles of bored members of the congregation and, dare I say it, the dreaded choirboys?

One of the types of inscriptions that, at present, we can only offer a number of theories for, but little in the way of hard evidence, are the numerous depictions of birds, beasts and fish that are liberally scattered across the walls of our churches. They are to be found in churches across the country, and in Europe, and can be everything from crude outline sketches to ornate and semi-realistic depictions. Sometimes, they are to be found clustered together in groups, like the deer images inscribed into the tower arch at Troston, or a single motif that appears out of place and out of context, such as the lonely and odd-looking bird carved into the north arcade at Westerham church in Kent. In all of these cases, though, the real problem is that there are perhaps too many possible explanations for these inscriptions, with no hard evidence really favouring one interpretation or another.

This excess wealth of possible interpretations is perhaps best exemplified with the various explanations for all of the inscriptions of birds that can be seen in our churches. Such images of birds are really quite common and can be found on the walls of great buildings such as

Norwich and St Albans cathedrals and York Minster, as well as on the walls of our more lowly parish churches. The Surrey churches of Caterham, Pyrford and Shere all have nice examples, as does that of Leighton Buzzard in Bedfordshire, Stetchworth in Cambridgeshire, Tittleshall in Norfolk and Worlington and Lidgate in Suffolk – to mention only a few. Only in the case of Stetchworth can any possible identification of the type of bird be hazarded, where at least one of the inscriptions appears to be an owl, with all of the rest tending to be shown as rather stylised. They are clearly birds, but are so stylised that they could be anything from a peacock to a pelican, a dove to a dodo.

The medieval world, and medieval art in particular, has no lack of bird imagery and symbolism. Some of the most obvious and often-depicted images show the birds of the Biblical stories, such as the dove released by Noah from the ark. However, the dove is also used as a symbol to represent the Holy Spirit in general, seen floating above the head of Christ in numerous manuscript illustrations and paintings, and commonly appearing in scenes of the Annunciation and Pentecost. This perhaps also links to the early-medieval belief that, at the time of death, the soul departed through the mouth in the form of a small bird; perhaps the upward flight of birds echoed the concept of the soul's journey to heaven. Birds are also used as recognised symbols of the saints, with one of the most common being the eagle of St John the Evangelist, still to be seen in medieval wall paintings as far afield as Little Witchingham in Norfolk and St David's Cathedral in Pembrokeshire. Specific birds such as the peacock are also common finds within the wider field of medieval art, sometimes regarded as a symbol of human vanity and sometimes, due to the eye motif found on the magnificent tail feathers, as a symbol of evil and the evil eye, with many people still believing it is incredibly unlucky to allow peacock feathers to enter a house. Within the wider area of folklore, many birds, particularly those of a dark colour, were considered to be bringers of ill tidings and bad omens. In certain noble families, such as the Arundels and even the Bishops of Salisbury, the appearance of certain birds were omens of an impending death. With such a wealth of possible interpretations, it is hardly surprising that it is extremely difficult to suggest exactly what any particular graffiti inscriptions may mean. In cases such as the birds found inscribed into the chapel of Norwich Castle keep, where each has a very clear cross or crucifix coming out of their backs, it is clear that they were more than simply a representation of a dove seen sitting on a nearby window ledge, and the temptation is to associate them with images of the Holy Spirit, but even this is uncertain.

In only a very few cases can we turn around and state, without fear of contradiction (probably), exactly what some of these unusual images are intended to signify, and even in these cases the interpretation can sometimes be obscure in the extreme. At Field Dalling church in north Norfolk, a very strange depiction of a bird can be found on one of the piers of the north arcade, although the church in general contains very little in the way of graffiti inscriptions. The bird appears to be sitting at the top of a luxuriant tree or bush, has an odd arrow symbol coming out of the top of its head, and the whole is surrounded by what appear to be two writhing snakes. At first glance, the inscription is strange in the extreme. However, it turns out that it isn't unique. The inscription appears to represent a very rare medieval allegory for the church, found in only a very few medieval manuscripts and known as the peridexion tree. The story is that the peridexion tree was to be found only in far-off India, and that it bore the most marvellously sweet fruit that attracted birds to its branches from far and wide. However, around the base of the tree lived a great dragon or serpent. The birds, as long as they stayed within the branches of the tree, were safe from the serpent but, at the moment they tried to leave, the beast would devour them. The allegory appears to be that the tree itself represented the church, and that the birds were the souls of the individual members of the church, feasting upon the spiritual fruits offered by their faith. As long as they remained faithful, and stayed within the safety of the church and its teachings, they would be safe from the Devil, represented by the serpent or dragon. However, should they stray from the path of orthodox faith then their souls, like the little birds, would fall prey to the forces of evil.

To discover such a rare medieval allegory on the walls of a remote church in North Norfolk is most certainly unusual, and it does rather suggest that the story of the peridexion tree was perhaps far more widely known than the tiny handful of surviving manuscript illustrations suggests. What is even more interesting is that, despite the fact that the church contains very little graffiti scattered across the walls, this image appears to have become the focal point for what little graffiti there is.

All around the image are to be found a whole series of devotional crosses and merchant's marks, suggesting that the image may well have been a particular focus for local devotion – in much the same way that a shrine, side altar or religious statue may have been. While it is certainly gratifying to be able to suggest a positive identification for one single piece of such graffiti, it still leaves some many hundreds of images that remain, at least for now, as entirely unexplained.

You may well have thought that some of the other imagery might have a little less complex symbolism than the bird inscriptions, and might perhaps be easier to explain. One of the most obvious candidates for this must be the large number of images and inscriptions of fish that are to be found on church walls. From a modern perspective, it would appear simple to suggest that the fish is an ancient Christian symbol that has long been associated with the church. Indeed, the fish symbol is still commonly used by evangelic Christians to this day. However, nothing within the exploration of early graffiti is ever so simple or straightforward. The fish is most certainly an ancient Christian symbol, and stretches right back to the very earliest days of the religion, when Christians were being persecuted under the Romans. It is traditionally believed that the fish motif was used as a covert symbol among believers, allowing them to identify their fellows. Known as the ichthys, it can still be seen adorning early Christian memorials and tombs. However, by the Middle Ages, this association between the faith and the symbol seems to have disappeared. While fish do turn up in some areas of medieval religious art – most notably swimming around the feet of images of St Christopher as he carries the Christ child across the river – there appears no specific link between the fish and the Christian faith. Why then, it may be asked, is it still so commonly associated with Christianity today? The answer to this actually lies not in the ancient past but in very recent decades and, in particular, to the early 1970s and the anti-Vietnam War movement. The ichthys – as a symbol of peaceful rebellion in the face of what was considered to be militaristic jingoism – was adopted by a number of anti-war protest groups and its popularity spread via the numerous rock festivals of the period. Within the space of a few years, it was being re-adopted by evangelical sections of the church as a connection between the modern movements and their ancient past.

Crude depiction of a fish, Troston, Suffolk

It is, therefore, pretty clear that most of the fish inscriptions to be found within our churches cannot be seen through modern eyes as simple expressions of faith. Certainly, fish were extremely important to the medieval economy and diet. Although most people today realise that the medieval church instituted Friday as a day of 'fast', upon which no meat could be eaten, most people don't realise that this was only one small part of the many rules laid down by the church with regard to diet. On a fast day, no flesh could be consumed, or animal products such as milk or cheese, except those of animals that were of the water rather than the land. Therefore, on fast days, the principle source of protein was fish. In England, this did include freshwater fish (and for very convoluted reasons, puffin, barnacle geese and beaver), but there was still a massive reliance upon smoked herring and mackerel. At various times throughout the Middle Ages, Wednesdays and Saturdays were also considered days of fasting, meaning that in devout households almost half the week saw no protein other than fish eaten. In addition, certain times of year such as Lent and Advent were also considered periods of fasting, which meant that, taken with the regular fish days, over half the year was officially spent reliant upon fish. There were, of course, exceptions, such as for the very young, the very old and those suffering from illness, and it most certainly wasn't unknown for wealthier households to manage to acquire exemptions from the regular rules. However, for most of society, fish would have played a much larger part in their diets, and been a key element in their survival, than it does today. Perhaps this, then, may explain some of the many fish to be found etched into the walls of churches such as Troston, Great Yeldham in Essex, Lacock Abbey in Wiltshire, Wiveton and Norwich Cathedral?

Of the other animals of the medieval world, both of the field and the hunt, they actually make far fewer appearances among the graffiti inscriptions than one might expect. The horse, which was the powerhouse of the medieval economy and without which farming would have been a near impossibility, is relatively rare. A superb example was recently discovered on the walls of Barton Turf church in Norfolk, shown in great anatomical detail – but it is clear that this particular example was no cart or plough horse. Indeed, the upper section of the inscription is now worn and a few surviving lines in the stonework suggest that it was once part of a much larger scheme, including an armoured rider. The same is also true of a number of beautifully executed inscriptions of horses at Little Paxton in Huntingdonshire, where the main image is actually shown to be wearing a riding bridle, a military-style elongated bit, and riding reins. Although the depiction of a horse located inside the tower at Ashwell church in Hertfordshire does not appear to ever have had a rider as part of the inscription, it appears unclear exactly when this horse may date from. Whatever the truth of the matter, it is the case that horses appear far less frequently than one might imagine. The same is true of some of the other animals that would have been common sights to members of the medieval congregation. Dogs are rare finds, as are hares and rabbits, although one rather lovely inscription from Sutton in Bedfordshire appears to show an eager long-eared hound in pursuit of a speedy-looking rabbit or hare. Even fewer still are the depictions of cats. An enigmatic little depiction from Limpsfield in Surrey is such a sketchy outline that there is some debate as to whether the whiskered creature is actually meant to depict a rat or a cat. However, there is certainly no mistaking the cat inscribed into the wall of St Albans Abbey. Curled up into a tight ball, with big eyes facing out from the wall, the contented-looking cat looks as though it would be happy to remain comfortably on the wall for another four or five centuries.

Beyond the birds, beasts and fishes there are many, many inscriptions to be found on the walls that, while being just as familiar to modern eyes, are also just as difficult to fully explain. Among the most common type of inscription, found everywhere from the lowliest parish church to the glory of Canterbury Cathedral, are the inscriptions and images of hands and feet. The hand impressions in particular, often drawn around a human hand itself, look hauntingly familiar to anyone who has seen early cave paintings. As a style of painting or image, they most probably go back to the very earliest days of Homo sapiens, when the need to leave a personal mark upon a wall, a mark to commemorate a life and existence, first emerged. And yet, many tens of thousands of years later, we find the exact same marks upon the walls of our medieval churches. Although these images of hands and feet do appear similar to the early cave paintings found across the world, there is indeed a medieval phenomenon that may offer an even closer parallel; that of the ex-voto items left by medieval pilgrims at shrines throughout England and the Continent.

The importance of pilgrimage in the Middle Ages really cannot be understated, serving both a spiritual function and offering many people a rare opportunity for travel and 'holy day' entertainment. As Chaucer's *Canterbury Tales* makes plain, pilgrimage was undertaken by all levels of medieval society, and the numbers involved can really be quite staggering. We can, with some confidence, record that 40,000 pilgrims passed through the gates of Munich on a single day in 1392, and that 142,000 arrived at Aachen on a single day in 1496. Although associated with particular festivals or offers of indulgence, which might make these figures somewhat atypical, popular shrines such as Wilsnack in northern Germany regularly received in excess of 100,000 pilgrims each year, which, for a town whose likely population was no more than 1,000, was an impressive feat of logistics. Similar popularity is shown at the major English shrines in the fifteenth century. Although exact numbers of pilgrims visiting the major shrines of St Thomas Becket at Canterbury and Our Lady of Walsingham in Norfolk are harder to establish, the revenues produced by these shrines, derived largely from pilgrims' offerings, suggest that they continued to attract very large numbers of pilgrims right up until the very eve of the Dissolution. Indeed, by the very end of the fifteenth century, the shrine at Walsingham, and the relatively new shrine of Henry VI at Windsor, were both generating an income over seven times that generated by the pilgrims to Canterbury. Beyond the offerings made at shrines, medieval pilgrimage was an industry in its own right. From the pilgrim trade came the very first written English guide books, known as 'itineraries', and a lucrative industry selling souvenir pilgrim badges, as well as numerous wayside hostelries that catered to the pilgrims' needs. However, the religious houses themselves made their money from offerings left by devout pilgrims, and a popular site could make a small fortune each year.

By far the most common form of offering, still seen in Catholic countries to this day, were images and models of parts of the body – often of the area that had been cured, or for which a cure was being sought. Eamon Duffy, in his monumental work on the English Reformation, *The Stripping of the Altars*, gives numerous accounts and instances of these ex-voto items, describing them as 'a standard part of the furniture of a shrine'. As well as acting as offerings and prayers of thanksgiving, these items advertised the particular saint's efficacy and power, and even as a visual reminder as to the specialisation that individual saints offered to certain maladies, in the same way that the signs outside medieval merchants' shops showed what you could expect to find within. As Thomas More recorded in his accounts of the shrine of St Valery in Picardy – who was regarded as being efficacious in matters relating to the sexual organs – 'all theyr offrynges that honge aboute the walles/none other thynge but mennes gere and womens gere made in waxe'. Contemporary accounts make it clear that the ex-voto offerings at the shrine of St Valery were unusual only in respect of what they depicted, although other recorded offerings were also perhaps a little out of the ordinary.

In 1285, it is recorded that Edward I had made an offering of wax candles at the church or St Mary, Chatham, of a total length equal to the combined heights of the royal family, and the following year sent a wax image of a sick gerfalcon to the shrine of St Thomas at Canterbury. More common, though, were the ex-voto offerings recorded as being present at many of the major shrines of Europe. Alongside the numerous chains and shackles of freed prisoners and crutches from healed cripples were many hundreds of wax models of hands, feet, limbs and heads, given by those who had received, or were seeking, a cure for their ailments. The numbers present at some shrines was so great that at least one pilgrim, visiting the popular shrine of Rocamadour, accused the monks of actually making them themselves. The wax that these ex-voto items were made of had many uses. In the first instance, the items were used to adorn the shrine. However, at the larger pilgrim centres, the number of these gifts meant that this wasn't possible, with only the more precious gifts being displayed. The wax was then either sold off to provide further income for the shrine, or melted down into candles to light the sacred spaces of the church, abbey or cathedral.

The parallels between the hand and feet graffiti inscriptions and the ex-voto items found at medieval shrines is striking. In addition, we do come across very large concentrations of these types of graffiti at sites that were known to be popular destinations for medieval pilgrims. Any visitor to Canterbury Cathedral need only look around the benches that line the medieval cloister to see literally hundreds of these inscriptions. The same can be said of the churches that make up the villages of the Glaven port in north Norfolk, which is thought to have been one of the main landing places for pilgrims travelling to the nearby shrine of Walsingham from the Continent. The font base at Morston church is still covered in dozens of foot inscriptions, many of which are clearly medieval in origin. However, it is also clear that pilgrimage cannot account for all the hand and foot inscriptions still being discovered across England. At sites such as Troston, the medieval plaster inside the porch, as well as areas of the tower arch, are covered in hand inscriptions. While some are clearly drawings that are simply meant to represent hands, others have very clearly been traced around actual hands themselves. The same is true at Litcham and Impington in Cambridgeshire, and yet none of these sites has any known particular association with pilgrimage. In addition to this, it has been noticed in recent years that the same types of medieval foot or shoe inscriptions are to be found carved into medieval bridges and wayside chapels, suggesting that the foot inscriptions may actually be offerings more associated with travel – which, of course, pilgrims were undertaking –

rather than the pilgrimage destination itself. Or, perhaps just as likely, it could well be a combination of the two.

The idea that many of these inscriptions were designed to act in the same way as ex-voto items raises a number of interesting questions and ideas. On the face of it, these inscriptions can be thought of as the cheap alternative to the traditional ex-voto item, for those who couldn't afford the small amount of wax that was needed to make one. However, as we have seen, even kings who could, and did, make offerings of immense value to English shrines were not averse to also making offerings of wax, which rather suggests that the financial value of an offering was not the main consideration. Indeed, the wax, once turned into candles, would, when burnt, carry the prayer straight up to heaven: a direct message to the Almighty. However, what the graffiti inscriptions do have, of course, is a sense of being permanent, and in this case, perhaps, that sense of permanence was actually seen as enhancing the potency of the offering. Once the candles had been burnt, once the last vestiges of wax had been scraped from the altar and the brief wisps of smoke dispelled by the breeze, the graffiti inscriptions would still be there. A permanent memorial to a faith that was as strong as the stone into which it was inscribed.

CHAPTER EIGHTEEN

THE MUSIC OF FAITH

Medieval musical notation and portrait, Lidgate, Suffolk

'As some to church repair, not for the doctrine, but the music there'

Alexander Pope, An Essay on Criticism I

The English Reformation in the sixteenth century took so much away from the church in terms of art and architecture that it is easy to overlook one of the most obvious and fundamental losses: that the music of the medieval church was gone for ever. The church in the Middle Ages was one that was bright with lively instruments, songs and plainchant, much of which was swept away by the reformers' zeal. That isn't to say that the church became a place of quiet solitude overnight, but, during the century following the Reformation, the austere whitewashed walls reflected a more austere approach to music within the church. The ritual chants and songs, the seasonal processions led by musicians around the parish and the echoing voices filling the stone vaults were to be driven out by the dull prescribed dirges of the Puritans, who, at least from a distant perspective, associated joyful celebration with sin. The fact that we have so much early-church music surviving today is to be celebrated, as it gives us a tiny glimpse into all that has been lost.

The importance of music in the regular life of the medieval church, in all its forms, cannot be overstated. The parish day, week, month and year was regulated by the services of the church, and each of these was invariably accompanied by music. Music gave each of those services both structure and form. Parish processions were led by musicians and no major event would pass by without music adding to the atmosphere. In the church itself, singing and chant were the order of the day, with musicians sometimes stationed around the church to make best use of the acoustics. It is even known that the gallery above the rood screen in some churches, and even the rood beam, had singers stationed there during certain services. As we will see, it wasn't unknown to have an entire organ installed in the rood loft, designed to carry music into every corner of the church. In the larger churches, groups of singing men and boys formed some of the earliest secular choirs, singing as much for their own enjoyment as for the church and the glorification of God. The medieval church has been described as an audio landscape of devotion, where the music added a depth of meaning and mystery to the purely visual; an audio-visual spectacle of everyday belief.

Among the graffiti inscriptions to be found in our churches are a remarkable number that relate to the early music of the medieval parish. The most common of these are depictions of musical instruments, of which the harp is found in greater numbers than all other types. Usually shown in a rather stylised manner, images of harps can be found everywhere from Exeter Cathedral to Bassingthorpe in Lincolnshire, with East Anglia boasting an unusually large number. Good examples are to be found at Morley St Peter in Norfolk, Shere in Surrey and Willingham, Sawston and Hardwick in Cambridgeshire. Although all these inscriptions clearly show the instruments, it is more than likely that at least some of them were created as symbols rather than accurate depictions of real harps. In the medieval church, the harp was associated with a number of saints, including Patrick, and was also deeply associated with angels and the concept of blessing. In many examples of medieval art, the harp was also associated with the biblical King David, and he was often depicted as sitting with a small harp upon his knees. However, as the examples of harp graffiti are so scattered across the country, with no obvious distribution pattern, it is impossible to suggest which harps may have been made to simply show a musical instrument and which were created as devotional symbols. It is only really at one church, Great Walsingham in Norfolk, that it is clear that there is a deeper meaning to the harp graffiti. In the late medieval porch of the church are to be found over half a dozen harp inscriptions, scattered across the stonework, ranging from the elaborate and neatly executed to hastily scratched marks that are mere outlines. With no obvious connections to the church dedication, and no records of a local family called Harp or Harper, it is still impossible to decide exactly what all these harps were meant to mean – but it is clear that they were meant to mean something.

Very occasionally, you may come across a graffiti depiction of far-rarer instruments than harps, instruments that have no obvious religious connotations and are, therefore, quite likely to have been inscribed purely as a representation of the instrument itself. At Parham church in Suffolk, the stones of the tower arch are quite literally covered in early-graffiti inscriptions, including numerous harps, ships, birds, people and text. However, despite the fine quality of the graffiti there, the most important inscriptions are actually two crudely made little pictures of medieval organs. Although neither inscription can really be regarded as great works of art, one of them does appear to contain quite a lot of information concerning the instrument itself. It is clear that the inscription is meant to represent a small, most probably portable, pipe organ set upon a stand. At the front it is also possible to make out a crude depiction of the actual keyboard, although the number of keys is far fewer than the number of pipes shown. The organ is obviously heavily associated with modern churches, but was far less so during the Middle Ages, when just about any instrument could be found making music within a parish church. However, from the fifteenth century onwards, such small organs begin to appear in increasing numbers in manuscript illustrations, most often shown as being played by angels. It's also at this period that notes concerning organs begin to appear in church-wardens' account books, suggesting that they are becoming increasingly common within our parish churches. The early-sixteenth-century accounts from St Michael's church in Spurriergate, York, state that there was an organ in the church when the accounts begin in 1518; but this was in a poor state of repair and was removed from the church in 1525, only to be replaced with a new small organ in 1527. However, the new organ simply wasn't up to the task and, in 1535, the parish paid for an organ maker to travel to York from London to build a new organ, which sat in the choir of the church. All this organ-related activity finally culminated in 1543, with the parish paying the handsome sum of 33s 4d to 'William the organ maker in Castlegate' to make an entirely new organ, to be installed in the rood loft.

The musical instruments may still be found carved into the walls of our churches, but very little is actually known about the people who played them. We find passing references to musicians and singers in parish accounts, and the odd very rare reference to 'mummers' or players – come to entertain at parish festivities – but for those who devoted their lives to making noise and entertainment, they are oddly silent. Few graffiti inscriptions appear to show musicians of any sort, despite their obvious presence within the church. At Benington in Lincolnshire, it is possible to make out a figure who is clearly playing a trumpet or horn of some kind, although he appears to be associated with another group of figures, most probably soldiers, dating to the sixteenth century. To date, it is only at Stoke-by-Clare in Suffolk that early musicians can be seen with any real clarity. Here are to be found two figures that appear to represent church musicians. The first is shown with his head thrown back and his mouth wide open, suggesting that he may be singing, while the second is clearly shown playing a four-hole pipe or shawm. Both wear identical hats, suggesting they were created by the same individual, and it would appear that they were originally not alone. There are a number of other now-badly degraded inscriptions in the church that appear very similar to the musicians, and the whole group may well have once represented a church band.

One of the most obvious types of music within the medieval parish, and one that would have been noticeable every single day of the year for the inhabitants of the parish, were the church bells. The tradition of church bells in England dates at least as far back as the Anglo-Saxon period, with the Venerable Bede recording that there was a bell at Whitby Abbey as long ago as the late seventh century. There is even archaeological evidence for the manufacture of large church bells, in the form of large casting pits, at both Winchester Old Minster and Gloucester, dating from the tenth century. By the time of the Norman Conquest, large bells were commonplace items within parish churches, and documents survive that talk about how they were to be rung and upon what occasion. The church bells would have rung out to warn villagers of the beginning of a service as well as upon special occasions. The fifteenth-century will of Jeffery Elyngham of Fersfield in Suffolk makes note that the church bells were rung to accompany parish processions, and accounts from Dereham in Norfolk indicate that the church clerks were paid 6d for ringing the bells during Easter week and upon the anniversary of the church benefactor's commemoration. The church bells would also mark the local events within the parish calendar, with ringing for weddings and the tolling of the bells for a death. Indeed, there was probably never a day that went by when an individual did not hear the church bells ring out across the parish at least once.

The village church bells, however, served much more of a purpose than just marking the services of the church. From the very earliest times, the bells themselves were seen to have special powers of blessing, and they were regarded as spiritual objects in their own right. There are many recorded cases of pilgrim badges, which functioned as a type of holy relic in their own right, actually being cast into the bells during their production, thereby passing on their own blessedness to the newly made bell. When the bells were installed within a church tower, they themselves were then blessed by a priest or bishop, sometimes known as the 'baptism of the bells', and, as far back as the thirteenth century, it was believed that the ringing of church bells drove away demons, as well as offering a blessing to all who were within earshot. In many parishes, it was the tradition to ring the church bells during thunderstorms, in the belief that the storms were the work of evil, and that the sound of the blessed bells would drive away such evil and therefore calm the storm. In 1552, the reformer Hugh Latimer preached against such practices, stating that 'if the holy bells would serve against the devil . . . no doubt we would soon banish him out of all England. For if all the bells in England should be rung together at a certain hour, I think there would be almost no place but some bells might be heard.' It is of course worth remembering that the ringing of church bells during a thunderstorm wasn't an entirely safe thing to do. It is recorded that in France, between the years 1753 and 1786, over a hundred bell ringers were actually killed holding onto rain-sodden bell ropes during lightning storms – leading to an eventual national ban. The records for medieval England are less forthcoming, but still suggest that the ringing of the bells to dispel storms was not without its hazards.

The importance of the sound of bells within the English parish is reflected in the graffiti of our churches, where all forms of bells are common discoveries. At Lindsey in Suffolk, Shillington in Bedfordshire, Girton in Cambridgeshire, Graveley in Hertfordshire and at Norwich Cathedral, images of bells are prominent among the local graffiti inscriptions, and perhaps reflect the place that church bells had in the everyday round of church services and belief. This belief was something that not even the English Reformation could wipe away with impunity. Despite the fact that the Reformation saw most churches lose all but one of their bells, the ringing traditions simply failed to die out. In the diocese of Lincoln, which stretched from the Humber to the Thames and was one of the largest in England, it had always been a tradition to ring the bells in honour of the Feast of St Hugh of Lincoln (17 November). Although, officially, this remained outlawed during the reign of Elizabeth I, 17 November just happened to be the queen's own Accession Day – which the good people of the diocese of Lincoln took to celebrating with the ringing of the church bells.

Beyond the instruments and musicians, the one area of graffiti that is most certainly and unequivocally related to music within the medieval church is the actual music itself. Very occasionally, inscriptions have been identified that are clearly representations of musical notation etched into the walls. To date, only a dozen or so of these inscriptions have been discovered, although more will undoubtedly come to light, making them one of the rarest type of graffiti inscription in the country. What is perhaps most notable about these inscriptions (pun intended) is that almost half of these have been discovered not in the thousands of parish churches scattered across the country, but in a handful of cathedrals and minsters. The probable reason for this apparent bias in distribution must be that it was in the larger cathedrals and minsters where music was actually written down. With the large-scale spectacle that revolved around cathedral services, and the high numbers of individuals involved, the music and singing formed a central part in their regular services. As a result, the music in a medieval cathedral was regulated and organised, and formal musical notation, most particularly in manuscript form, was common. It is no coincidence that many modern cathedrals still have a singing school, and officers responsible for music, as part of the establishment. At the individual parish level, the creation, teaching and learning of music would likely be much more informal, with the more experienced musicians and vocalists passing on their skills to the novices by direct teaching and example. Musical manuscripts would appear to have been rarities, or at least few survive, and it is actually quite unlikely that, had they been present, many of the parish musicians would have been able to understand them. Even today, the ability to read music is certainly not universal, and this ability is likely to have been far less widespread during the Middle Ages. As a result, musical graffiti is found largely in the places where written music was commonplace.

Some of the finest examples of musical graffiti are to be found in our most notable medieval cathedrals and abbeys. Neatly executed musical notation has been recorded in the nave of Norwich Cathedral and St Albans Abbey. At York Minster, meanwhile, there are two superbly cut examples in the passageway that leads between the Chapter House and the north transept, suggesting perhaps that this area was either used for musical practice, or was an area where those with musical knowledge found themselves waiting with time on their hands. The fact that one of the examples is clearly unfinished, and that both are to be found near the benches that run along the walls, might suggest that the latter explanation is perhaps more likely. There are also two very neatly done examples, now in Wells Museum, that were inscribed into fragments of slate and excavated from the site of the former Manor of Mudgley in Somerset. The manor was once the property of the Dean and Chapter of Wells Cathedral, and the slates may well have been used as musical teaching aids. The examples found in the smaller parish churches tend to be rather less formal and neat in their execution than those found in the cathedrals. Where the staves of the cathedral graffiti may look as though they had been drawn with a straight edge, most of those found in the parish churches are most certainly freehand. The musical inscriptions to be found at Horning, Lidgate, Ashwell, Willingham, and Rayleigh in Essex, are all clearly created by individuals with a good understanding of musical notation. However all – with the possible exception of Lidgate – appear to be rather hasty and haphazard interpretations.

The inscriptions at Lidgate are unique among all the examples of musical graffiti, in that it is clear that they were never meant to be played. There are three musical inscriptions in the church, all slightly different, but each, rather than being just a series of musical notes, form part of larger inscriptions. These inscriptions are all designed to be read as a word puzzle, or rebus, and each contain a mixture of letters, musical notes on a four-bar stave, and an image. The inscriptions appear to date back to the early fifteenth century and, although they have been known about for some decades, it took a group of scholars from Cambridge University to finally unravel their meaning. The inscriptions begin in a straightforward manner, with the letters 'W E L L'. These are followed by four musical notes set upon a stave, the letters 'D Y', and then an image of what appears to be a dice or die. The puzzle concludes with the letters 'Y N E'. The musical notes have been identified as representing solfège, a musical teaching system that applies a syllable to each note and which dates back at least as far as the eleventh century. Looked at in this light, the four notes appear to represent 'fa', 're', 'mi' and 'la'. The rest of the rebus suddenly makes sense when you understand that the common medieval term for a dice was a cater, leaving the whole inscription to read 'Well fare mi Lady Cateryne' ('Well fare my Lady Catherine'). We will probably never know the true identity of the individual who created the inscription – or Lady Catherine, for that matter – but they must have been a well-educated person, comfortable enough with both music and letters to be able to create such a pun. There is also disagreement about the actual meaning of the message. Was it a note of good wishes or a message of love and longing? Whoever they were, and whatever the original meaning of the message, they have left their mark on both Lidgate church and history.

The dating of these examples of musical notation should, you would think, be relatively straightforward. Many of what appear to be the earliest examples, such as those from Norwich, Horning and York, all appear written on a four-line stave, rather than the more usual five-line stave that we use today. The four-line stave was used throughout the later Middle Ages for most forms of musical notation, only being generally replaced by the five-line stave in the sixteenth century. The five-line stave, it is generally believed, was a French import that soon became generally accepted throughout England. Therefore, music written on a four-line stave should be dated to before the middle of the sixteenth century. However, as with dating all types of graffiti inscriptions, nothing is ever quite so straightforward. It transpires that the changeover from the four-line stave to the five-line stave was not a simple and all-encompassing transition. The four-line stave continued in use – and continues in use until the present day – when writing particular types of 'chant' music. As most of the music used within the medieval-church setting was indeed chant music, it suddenly becomes clear that much of the musical graffiti need not necessarily belong to the medieval period. However, despite this slight setback, there are a number of examples that, based upon their surroundings and context, we can clearly date back to the later Middle Ages.

The Prior's Chapel at Durham Cathedral today forms parts of the deanery, and is rightly famous for the spectacular array of medieval wall paintings that it contains. The chapel itself was most probably built in the thirteenth century, although subsequent remodelling of the buildings means that it has been much altered over the years. The wall paintings that survive are actually the result of one of the later alterations to the building and, from the style of dress and costume, they have been reasonably securely dated to around the time 1460 to 1470. However, the scheme was painted onto a thin layer of limewash that has been quite badly damaged as a result of later alterations to the building – in places, the paint scheme has been lost, revealing the earlier wall surface beneath. On this surface can be seen evidence of an earlier painted scheme and across the surface of these earlier wall paintings, scratched into the plaster beneath, are a whole mass of graffiti inscriptions. All of these inscriptions must have been created before the later paint scheme was completed. The inscriptions contain just about every type of graffiti you would expect to see in a medieval religious building. Alongside consecration crosses there are other compass-drawn designs, ragged staffs, a wild boar, harps, plants, a heraldic achievement of arms and a great deal of medieval text. In addition, the graffiti contains at least one section of musical notation, clearly set out on a four-line stave. The music in the Prior's Chapel is particularly significant as we may even have some idea of who was likely to have created it. The documentary records for the cathedral show that the secular singing men, who were employed to sing at services but were not part of the monastic community, were using the Prior's Chapel as a rehearsal space. They had been forced to vacate the cathedral's Chapter House after their singing led to numerous complaints – rather suggesting that they had a need to practice. Perhaps the musical graffiti that still sits upon the wall of the chapel represents a piece that they were working on at some point back in the fifteenth century, and long after all memory of them has gone, their music still sits, unfinished, on the walls.

CHAPTER NINETEEN

DEATH STALKS THE WALLS

Small demon and shoe outline, Troston, Suffolk

'Mors computatur umbre que semper sequitur corpus'
(Death may be likened to a shadow which always follows the body)

Inscription in Gamlingay church, Cambridgeshire

The distribution of graffiti around churches may, at first glance, appear fairly random. However, there are certain patterns that have been shown to exist. These patterns certainly can't be found in every church, but they exist in enough examples to begin to be sure that they are not a mere figment of the imagination or statistical fluke. In general terms, more graffiti will be found in the nave than the chancel, the latter being the area reserved for the priest and notable patrons of the church. Likewise, the upper areas of the tower are likely to be full of graffiti created by the bell ringers – a practice that continues unabated to this day. Within the nave there also seems to be a strong likelihood of graffiti concentrations being found near the doorway or entrance and around the area of the font. Porches and the stonework surrounding the main south door also show distinct concentrations, or hot spots, for graffiti inscriptions. It is arguable, though, that more graffiti survives in porches because they are now regarded as less important than they were in the Middle Ages and are, therefore, a lot less likely to have suffered from overzealous restoration. As with all patterns, there are also obvious exceptions to the rule. At Troston church, there is actually very little graffiti in the nave, but a massive amount found in the chancel. Exactly why such churches contradict the usual patterns is, at the moment, something of a mystery.

Just as there are certain places around a church where you are more likely to find graffiti inscriptions than elsewhere, there are also certain periods of time when graffiti appears to have been far more likely to have been created than at other times. These chronological hot spots are not at first obvious, tending to be a far more scattered phenomena that only becomes noticeable after looking at a number of sites, but they are most certainly present. The most easily recognisable of these hot spots are the most recent ones, and the dates inscribed with them tend to be a bit of a giveaway. These include the period 1939–45, 1914–18, the early decades of the nineteenth century and the middle of the seventeenth century – all, of course, representing times of either national conflict or serious social unrest. Second World War graffiti has already been subject to a number of surveys that have attempted to record many of the more temporary graffiti inscriptions, often created in pencil, on buildings and structures that are fast being swept away from the countryside. These inscriptions have proved a fruitful area of investigation for social historians, particularly looking at the hopes and fears of the common soldier, sailor or airman.

Exactly why graffiti inscription should be more likely to be created during these periods is still a little open to debate. In terms of the Second World War graffiti, it can be argued that those years saw a massive number of men and women moved away from their normal routines and familiar surroundings, and with a constant threat hanging over their existence, making it an act of memorial or remembrance; a mark left upon the present created by a fear that there would be no tomorrow. This can certainly be argued to be the case for much of the air-force graffiti scattered across the east of England in churches, pubs and barrack rooms. The Crown Hotel in Downham Market, Norfolk, was a popular pub with members of the local bomber squadrons from RAF Marham and its satellite station at Bexwell for much of the war. The young bomber crews were among the RAF's elite, and formed a part of the Pathfinder group – the expert crews sent over an enemy target before the main body of bombers to clearly mark the intended target. The job was a risky one and, as a result, casualties were high. The pilots and their crews who drank in the Crown Hotel knew that the odds were stacked against them. To this day, there remains in the bar a small elm-wood table, polished and darkened by generations of spilt beer and elbows, into which the bomber crews etched their names. The surface, once a mass of writing, has now faded, until only a few dozen names can be clearly made out. Until very recent years, veterans would return to the bar to point out their inscribed name to children or grandchildren, sip a half or two of local bitter, and stare long and hard at the names of those who never made it home.

This need to memorialise may well be the main factor behind much of the graffiti created during these periods of unrest and conflict, and it is certainly the easiest to rationalise. However, other factors may also be at play here. While a need to leave a record of one's own existence has a certain personal resonance, it may well be that people felt the need to record and document the events themselves. Diaries, letters and written accounts of all these periods are relatively commonplace, and the more modern the event the more likely it is that these have survived. However, such survivals can never be taken for granted, and the fact that such documents would survive may have appeared far from obvious, or even likely, to those people who actually lived through these terrible and terrifying events. The very act of inscribing the stonework of a building, particularly a building that has stood for many centuries, could well have appeared as a far more permanent and unshakable record for the future. When papers and documents were every day being lost to the flames and destruction, the inscribing of ancient stonework may well have had an attraction.

This idea of graffiti acting as a more permanent memorial to events is actually supported by a good number of surviving medieval inscriptions, and most particularly those relating to some of the most devastating and traumatic events of the Middle Ages. The most obvious such event, known to every schoolchild in England, was the Black Death of 1349. Although never known as such at the time, being referred to simply as the 'pestilence', it was the greatest and most devastating of a whole series of plagues that regularly visited medieval England, carrying off countless men, women and children. These are the types of events that were of such a catastrophic nature that, for those who lived through them, it would have been all too easy to see them as the end of all things, the destruction of the world and society that they had known all their lives. As they had seen, the everyday world of written records, manor courts and parish order could fall away completely in a matter of weeks. The ordered medieval world could fall into chaos, with houses standing empty and crops mouldering unharvested in the fields, highlighting just how fragile existence was, and how narrow the line that was drawn between survival and the grave, order and anarchy.

It is difficult to imagine the horror of this event on a national level, difficult to visualise just what the loss of between a third and a half of the nation's population would really have been like to witness, to be a part of. The example of a single rural village, where written records give names of individuals and families, is perhaps easier to grasp – and perhaps more horrific in its detail. In the Suffolk village of Lakenheath, the plague didn't arrive until early in 1349, having already ravaged the southern counties of England since it first appeared at Weymouth in June 1348. Indeed, the northward spread of the disease appeared to have come to a halt late the previous year, just as it reached Suffolk's southern border on the river Stour, and the villagers of Lakenheath must have prayed that they had been spared. Sadly, it was not to be. In January of 1349, a new outbreak of the disease appeared in north-western Suffolk. This time there was to be no escape, with the first reported cases in early January actually being from Lakenheath itself. The village acted as a modest inland port and it is likely that the disease, as it did all over the rest of Europe, followed the inland commercial waterways. Within a few weeks the manor courts, the administrative machinery of village life, had been suspended until further notice, with the last court, held in February, indicating that over twenty of the most prominent landholders in the parish were already dead. How many women and children were dead by this time is unknown, they being deemed too unimportant to feature in the official record. Then, in late February, the written records all cease. The spring passes in silence, with the blanket of death laid thick upon the voices of the medieval parish. The days, weeks and months of suffering and death have left no mark. A blank period. By the time the records begin to reappear, in late May, it is clear that about half of the parish, including the old parish priest and his subsequent replacement, had fallen to the plague during the late winter and early spring. Entire families disappear from the parish records, with new prominence given to others, such as the soon-to-be-well-off Mann family, who had barely rated a mention only a few short months before. Between February and May, the village of Lakenheath had seen the established order of countless generations swept aside as the Devil had stalked through their parish.

What is perhaps most surprising, particularly after the events of 1348–49, is that the world did not fall into complete and irrevocable chaos. It faltered perhaps, a short suspension to the daily, weekly and seasonal routines, but, in a matter of only a few short years, normality – albeit with a few altered ground rules – had returned. But for the people living through those months, watching as friends, family and neighbours each fell in turn to the pestilence, it must have seemed as though the chances of such normality ever returning were slim indeed.

That the end of all things was upon them, and the world would never be the same again. As a result, the idea of recording such events in parchment just wasn't enough. It was just too impermanent, and people's need to record such events for posterity, to leave their mark upon this world that was collapsing about them, was just too great. They turned instead to the one place that they had always traditionally turned when looking to memorialise a life, a deed or a good intention: they turned to the parish church.

The best-known graffiti inscription relating to the plague years of the mid-fourteenth century is to be found in Ashwell church. The church itself is full of graffiti inscriptions from the Middle Ages, including architectural inscriptions, biblical texts, ritual protection markings, jibes at the local archdeacon and the odd piece of heraldry. However, it is one inscription in the tower that has long captured the attention of both visitors and medieval scholars. It reads as:

Pestile (n) cia

M.C.T.(er)x penta

miseranda ferox violenta

(discessit pestis) superset plebs pessima testis in fine qevent(us)

(erat) valid(us)

(. . . h)oc anno maurus in orbe tonat MCCCLXI

Which can be translated as:

There was a plague

1000, three times 100, five times 10,

a pitiable, fierce violent

(plague departed); a wretched populace survives

to witness and in the end

a mighty wind, Maurus, thunders in this year

in the world, 1361

The inscription is dated 1350, and clearly refers, at least in the first section, to the pestilence that fell upon the parish the preceding year. However, it is also clear that, for Ashwell at least, the Black Death was seen as only one in a number of devastating events that they felt the need to record in the fabric of the parish church. The inscription also refers to the great storm of St Maur's day (15 January) 1361, which tore down church towers and lay waste to forests across England, another event that would have piled further woes upon a community only just recovering from the effects of the great plague. These devastating events, which had far-reaching consequences that would echo down the generations, were recorded in the fabric of the one building that, by its very permanence, anchored the community in both the past and the future. Long after the unknown author of the text had followed the inevitable route of death and corruption, the inscription would stand as a testament to the horrors that had gone before. Sadly, it isn't just at Ashwell that such inscriptions are to be found. At the church of St Edmund in Acle, a lengthy inscription was uncovered in the chancel during restoration work in the early twentieth century and, thanks to the quick thinking of both the builders and rector, it has been preserved for posterity. Unusually, the Latin inscription was drawn in charcoal onto the wall plaster, making its survival all the more miraculous. The text begins:

Nota. O mors mesta nimis, quamplures mergis in imis.
Nunc hose, nunc illos, nunc rapis undique, mors . . .

It translates as:

Oh, lamentable death,
how many dost though cast in to the pit!
Anon the infants fade away,
and of the aged death makes an end.
Now these, now those, thou ravagest,
o death on every side;
Those that wear horns or veils, fate spareth not.
Therefore, while in this world the brute
beast plague rages hour by hour,
With prayer and with remembrance
deplore death's deadliness.

The Acle inscription tells tale of a community in crisis. The old and young are taken, and the pestilence respects neither the godly nor the sinner. All fall before the illness and all the parish has to fall back upon is prayer. The inscription itself, though, most probably doesn't refer to the time of the Black Death in the middle of the fourteenth century, as the text appears to be somewhat later in style, and it probably relates to one of the many smaller outbreaks that occurred throughout the fifteenth century. Nevertheless, the effects of even such smaller-scale plagues had obviously devastating effects upon villages such as Acle.

However, of all the graffiti inscriptions that attempt to record the plague, to make note of its passing like a scythe through their own parish, the most chilling and emotive must be that from Steeple Bumpstead in Essex. Here the inscription isn't of the memorialising and narrative style found at Ashwell or Acle, but a much more personal account of a devastation that was ripping through a parish in despair. Dated 1348, the year that the Black Death or 'pestilence' first entered England, the inscriptions simply read, 'God help me' – and are repeated in several places around the pillars of the church. Once the viewer understands the significance of the date inscribed upon the piers of the church, the message itself, albeit brief, tells us everything that we may wish to know. Its despair and brevity are eloquent testimony to a community facing what must have appeared to be the very end of the world as they knew it.

The accounts of the plagues that ravaged the country, and the church inscriptions they caused to be left behind at places such as Ashwell, Steeple Bumpstead and Acle have already been noted. However, there are other inscriptions that litter our church walls and tell stories of loss and grief. These inscriptions may not talk of deaths on the monumental scale of the plague, but their sheer intimacy and immediacy cuts deep to the quick. They talk not of devastation and a disruption of parish life, but of the loss of only one person – a father, mother, sister or brother – whose passing caused no less a ravaged hole in the hearts of those left behind. Some are more matter of fact than others, such as that from Horley in Surrey that just reads '*Hic jacet Barthome (Bartholemew) Saleman*' (Here lies Bartholemew Saleman) who, it must be assumed, was buried near the pillar upon which the inscription sits. Other inscriptions are more the nature of requests, such as that from Harlton in Cambridgeshire which asks the viewer to '*Orate pro anima Thoma Caius anime propicietur Deus amen*' (Pray for the soul of Thomas on whose soul God have mercy). A few miles away at Sawston, the inscription takes on a more pleading nature. The name Watton is inscribed in several places across the pillars of the church, and one such inscription is accompanied by the text '*miserere mei deus*' (may God have mercy upon); unfortunately, no Watton has so far been identified in the parish records.

Perhaps the most heartbreaking inscriptions to discover are those that refer to long-dead children. These really shouldn't be anything of a surprise, with medieval infant mortality rates being so much higher than today. It has been suggested that about a third of all medieval infants perished before they were five years old, and perhaps as many as five per cent of adult females died during childbirth, with a significant percentage dying later of subsequent complications and infection. However, in such cases, the stark facts and percentages mean very little. The death of a child would always be a blow to both friends and family, no matter how hardened you became towards sudden loss. For the lower orders in particular, where the loss meant a simple burial and the encouragement to move on with their lives, a child may pass and leave nothing behind but a few fleeting memories. For them, there would be no memorial brass, no gravestone or monumental plaque; no reminder of a short life lived. For some members of the parish, it appears that this was not enough – and they, too, decided to leave a more permanent memorial etched into the walls of the parish church. At Gamlingay, a tiny inscription in the north aisle reads, '*Hic est sedes margaratea vit an d(ecimo)*' (Here lies Margaret in her tenth year). A few miles away at Kingston, a worn inscription appears to tell of an even more tragic tale.

The Maddyngley family were an old Kingston family. There had been Maddyngleys in the village since at least as far back as 1279, when a Robert Maddyngley is recorded as one of the tenant farmers associated with lands held by Kingston Wood manor, the largest of the village's manor holdings. The records, such as they are, suggest a family of neat respectability who did not have a great deal of material wealth, and worked hard for what little they had; a typical yeoman family that formed the backbone of English medieval society. They only rarely turn up in the parish records, suggesting that they simply carried on with their lives as best they could, causing no undue disturbance to the fabric of parish life. The church in Kingston, though largely rebuilt after a disastrous fire in 1488, shows no sign of them ever having existed in the village; that is, until the dark days of 1515. In that year, yet another great pestilence began to spread its way across England. It began in London in the early spring, causing the court and nobility to scatter to their country estates, and there were fears that it was another outbreak of the lethal 'sweating sickness'. The 'sweats' or 'English sweats' was a strange disease that, according to tradition, only appeared during the reigns of the male Tudor monarchs. It had first appeared shortly after Henry Tudor's victory at the battle of Bosworth – quite possibly actually imported into England by his foreign mercenaries – and then appeared with monotonous regularity almost every decade for the next fifty or sixty years. As diseases go, it was a terrible one, and remains largely not understood even today, and appears to have been both rapid in its onset and hugely deadly. The old saying was that a victim could be well at dinner time and dead by supper. However, in 1515, it turned out that it was not the 'sweat' that ravaged the countryside but the good old-fashioned bubonic plague.

In some respects, for the effect this outbreak had on London and the south-east of England, the disease might just as well have been the sweating sickness. Although the plague was usually a little less deadly than the sweating sickness, and had a higher recovery rate, this outbreak appears to have been particularly virulent. Oxford and Cambridge Universities suspended all studies, the courts were disbanded and places of gathering closed in an effort to stop its spread – but to little avail. Part of the problem was that this outbreak came only a short time after the last major outbreak of the 'sweats' in 1507. As was typical of the period, the years immediately after a major epidemic usually saw an increased birth rate, as families and communities tried to make good the losses of the previous pestilence. However, in the case of the 1515 epidemic, all this meant was that, when the plague began to ravage its way across England, the country had a far higher proportion of infants than it might ordinarily have – and it was these children who appear to have fallen victim to it in their hundreds and thousands. Across the south-east of England, they died, hastily buried in unmarked graves with little or no time to memorialise or remember them. In London, only the funeral processions, made up of just a few souls, walked the deserted streets, and in Kingston, a small village in rural Cambridgeshire, a memorial was left.

Cut neatly into the stonework, are three names – Cateryn Maddyngley, Jane Maddyngley and Amee Maddyngley. Exactly how old they were, we will probably never know, but the fact that they don't turn up as adults in the parish records rather suggests that all three were children or infants; all three related by blood. However, if the rest of the brief inscription is to be believed, the one thing we do know is that all three died in the same year: 1515. That same year a stolid, unremarkable tenant farmer quietly etched the names of his three dead children into the walls of the parish church, the only surviving proof that they were born, lived, died and were loved.

CHAPTER TWENTY

THE REFORMATION AND BEYOND . . . A BIT

Post-medieval graffiti, Norwich Cathedral

'Weep, weep, O Walsingham
Whose days are nights,
Blessings turned to blasphemies,
Holy deeds to despites.
Sin is where Our Lady sat,
Heaven is turned to hell.
Satan sits where Our Lord did sway;
Walsingham, O, farewell'

The Wracks of Walsingham, C16th

Henry VIII's split away from the Church of Rome and the establishment of the Church of England was probably one of the most monumental changes that English society had undergone in over five hundred years. Although it didn't have the immediate impact of foreign wars, disastrous famines or mass epidemics, it was to have more of a long-term impact on the everyday lives of individual people and their parishes than any other single event in centuries. After all, whether afflicted by warfare, famine or pestilence, the usual rounds of the day-to-day parish life soon struggled back to the centuries-long routine that they had always followed. Many of the individuals may have gone – and, in the case of the Black Death of the mid-fourteenth century, that meant approximately a third of the entire population of England – but the old routines, ceremonies and traditions of the church, and the parish it served, soon re-established themselves. The medieval year was governed by the feasts, festivals and saint's days of the church, and parish life was bound up with the calendar of the church. Even after the most terrible tragedies had befallen the nation, watches for the dead still took place, the ceremonial uncovering of the church rood at Easter still happened amid solemn ritual, Rogationtide perambulations still wended their way around the parish boundaries and candles were still lit before the coloured images of the saints. The same, though, cannot be said after the Reformation.

Those few decades in the middle of the sixteenth century did far more than strip our parish churches of their imagery, wealth and finery. Quite simply, those few short years stripped away five centuries of tradition and ritual that left the English church almost unrecognisable to those from even a single generation earlier. Certainly, the physical appearance of the parish church changed, robbed of its ornaments, stripped of its stained glass and with the bright wall paintings covered in layers of limewash. Its glorious rood screens were defaced, the teeth of rough saws bit deep into elegant medieval woodcarvings and its alabaster statues were shattered into so many meaningless fragments of rough stone. However, the destruction wrought by the Reformation went far deeper than the confiscation and smashing of pretty things; far beyond the wanton vandalism of the faith-blinded religious fanatic. While the physical destruction of works of art and wonder, memorials and memories, was obvious to all, it was the gradual and deliberate erosion of a way of life that was to eventually bite hardest and deepest. The Reformation stripped the parish of its established yearly round of festivals and holidays. It cast aside centuries-long traditions, and eased aside inconvenient and unfashionable beliefs. It ripped apart the life of the congregation and parish in such a way as to ensure that there would be no recovery, no return to the old ways. The religious reformers of the mid-Tudor court thought not in terms of evolution, but rather of revolution. The structure of tradition and familiar ceremony was, in their eyes, the underpinning to a morally and spiritually corrupt institution that had twisted the word of God to its own ends. Put simply, to sweep away the corruption of the Roman church, it was first necessary to sweep away the rituals and traditions that had for many centuries maintained them. To bring down the building, they had to pick away, piece by piece, at the foundation stones.

And there were rather a lot of pieces to pick away at. Beyond the painted images of saints and the bright glass were generations of deeply held beliefs and customs. The big ideas, such as a belief in purgatory for the souls of the departed, were bound up with a multitude of personal and parish-based customs; customs and rituals that stood squarely in the way of a reformed church. If any single year can be said to have been the tipping point for the Reformation, it was 1549. It was a year of unrest and brutal bloodshed across England, with rebellions in almost every county in the kingdom, and the use of foreign mercenaries to put down the commoners with unprecedented brutality. However, the real revolution was made up of smaller things; the little changes that, taken individually, meant little enough, but taken as a whole transformed the spiritual landscape of England. For the reformers it was a year that saw the culmination of years of effort and planning. For the English people it was a watershed. That one year saw the introduction of the Book of Common Prayer, with English superseding Latin as the language of the church, and whole services and dozens of saintly holidays being expunged from the calendar, the destruction of the chantries and charities of almost every settlement in the land – and the introduction of a law that finally made it acceptable for priests to marry. While each individual change may have had only a limited impact, taken together the ripples soon became a flood. The calendar of tradition and custom that had formally regulated the parish year lay in tatters and the parish priest, the very guardian of that parade of ritual devotion, was suddenly speaking English in church and marrying his housekeeper.

With these rituals and traditions also went the social structure of the medieval world, the guilds, chantries and charities established by countless generations to help their fellow parishioners. The effects were to reverberate down the centuries, leaving small echoes that can still be heard to this day. However, unlike the drama and immediacy of a famine or pestilence, the Reformation moved slowly, glacier-like and unstoppable, through two generations, leaving those few who did oppose it to simply wish for a return to the church as it was in our grandfather's time. While the events of 1549 may have marked a watershed that did result in uprising and bloody revolt, they were merely a confined reaction to changes that had been put in motion years beforehand.

Once the Reformation was well and truly underway, there was no going back. Even after the brief revival of the old ways under Mary I, her death saw them merely fall away again, no more than hollow echoes of what once was. Like the elderly soldier Sir Thomas Smythe, who at the end of the century was arguing for a return of the longbow to English armies, it was a lamentation for something that was already becoming a memory. Too much had gone, too much had been stripped away; like the smashed alabaster statues of the saints, the old traditions, customs and beliefs were simply too broken to repair. The world had already changed, the glacier of reform had already passed across the churches of England, leaving a newborn Church of England among the moraine. This disjuncture in English society, this stutter in the annual parish round of custom and belief, is also still evident upon the walls of our churches. Alongside the gouged-out faces of the saints, and the eyeless gaze of desecrated angels, the graffiti of the English parish church underwent a quite dramatic and fundamental change at the time of the Reformation.

Like the Reformation itself, the shift in graffiti content and style appears to have been a relatively gradual one, slowly shifting as the sixteenth century moved to a close. One of the most notable changes, as previously mentioned, was that dates began to appear with increasing regularity in graffiti inscriptions. Although there are a handful of medieval-dated inscriptions, they don't start to appear on a regular basic until the middle of the sixteenth century, and only become commonplace in the opening decades of the seventeenth century. In similar vein, the other most notable feature in the graffiti that appears after the Reformation is the general shift away from devotional inscriptions. The Latin prayers, ritual protection markings and votive images largely disappear from the walls, to be replaced by graffiti that is far more secular in nature and, in many respects, very similar to much of the street art and graffiti that we see today. It becomes more territorial and memorial in nature, very much in the vein of 'I was here', and appears to relate to the church as a building only, a surface in which to inscribe the design, rather than a place of spirituality or worship.

New types of graffiti begin to appear. The most obvious is the simple memorial graffiti, which subsequently becomes one of the most common types of graffiti found in churches and elsewhere. One such type of inscription, which seems to be fairly universal in its distribution, takes the form of a small house-shaped plaque, most usually containing initials and a date. These can be found just about everywhere that early graffiti is present, with the earliest dating back to the middle of the sixteenth century. Looking rather like little houses with a steeply pointed roof, these inscriptions have been interpreted as unfinished windmills, churches and even ale-houses. Sometimes the house shape will have a cross, or crosses, on the top, at others it will be a fleur-de-lis, but all invariably contain a date and initials. These enigmatic inscriptions do not appear to be associated with any other particular types of inscriptions and are often found in small groups. At the present time, there really isn't any clear consensus as to what they actually mean. The initials and dates can easily be regarded as some form of memorial graffiti; an inscription commemorating a visit, perhaps. However, the fact that there are many hundreds of these inscriptions, spread all over the country, and that all involve the same small house-like shape, leads to a number of questions: What exactly are the house shapes meant to represent? Why do they suddenly, it seems, become a universal type of graffiti? What, if anything, are their origins? There are of course a number of theories.

One is that these small plaques are monuments for the dead and recently departed, looking like small gravestones carved into the walls. Given that each contains only a set of initials and a date, and that the time period in which they begin to appear also generally corresponds with the time when churchyard gravestones and wall-mounted monuments also begin to appear, it is most certainly possible. However, superficial research at sites where some of these have been found has failed so far to establish a clear link. If these inscriptions do indeed relate to a death then the initials they contain should also tie in with names in the parish register of burials. While there are a few possible matches at some churches, the majority cannot be matched to the burial records. However, as I mentioned previously, the detailed research into this area has yet to be fully undertaken, and many more matches may yet come to light.

That is not, of course, to say that many of the graffiti inscriptions found in a medieval church context, and most particularly the ritual protection markings, suddenly stopped. They were simply too deep rooted in local custom and belief to be swept away by a mere Reformation of the church. Certain of the markings, most particularly the 'VV' symbols, do continue to be found in churches, spread across everything from the stonework to the woodwork. The other markings, the compass-drawn designs and other ritual-protection markings also continue. However, they appear to move out of the church and into the dwelling houses of the parishioners themselves. Anyone who has ever taken a close look at the timbers of a sixteenth- or seventeenth-century house, particularly the beam above the fireplace, is likely to have seen these self-same markings etched into the wood. The Reformation church, casting aside the 'superstitions', as they saw them, of the medieval Catholic faith, couldn't entirely stamp out the beliefs of countless generations. All it could do was move those beliefs out of the churches, where they would be frowned upon, into the privacy of the Tudor household.

While the post-Reformation church graffiti is very different in many respects from the medieval graffiti, it doesn't mean that it is any less interesting, or that it has less to tell us about the past. On the contrary, the common inclusion of dates from the middle of the sixteenth century actually means that many of these precisely dated inscriptions can tell us details of past events that simply don't appear elsewhere; events that don't make their way into the traditional written record. At Litlington church in Cambridgeshire, an intriguing little inscription is to be found by the window in the Lady Chapel. Although the original is in Latin, it reads as, 'Francis Drake, Knight, about to set sail in the thirty seventh year of the reign of the most august and serene prince, Elizabeth, Queen, by the grace of God, of England, France and Ireland, Defender of the faith, 1595 – the same always, John Sherman, April the tenth.' The inscription refers to Francis Drake's last ill-fated expedition to harry the Spanish, in which both Drake and his fellow leader, John Hawkins, succumbed to illness and died. John Sherman has been identified as a local landholder of some status, and it appears possible that his son-in-law, Robert Bownest, may actually have been a member of one of the twenty-seven crews that took part in the expedition. The local evidence suggests that, if he was involved, then Bownest actually survived the voyage, albeit suffering financial losses that forced him to sell much of his land only a few years later.

Similarly, on the right-hand side of the entrance to the tower at Lidgate church in Suffolk is a fascinating inscription that tells us a little about the local preparations for the defence against the Spanish Armada. The inscription begins with the initials 'TS' and the date '18th January 1583', in the twenty-sixth year of the reign of Elizabeth I, and states that a muster was held 'at this town'. A military muster was the gathering-together of all the men of the local militia force to undergo training, and was never an entirely popular activity in Tudor England. Not only did it take men away from their families and employment, quite often for several days, it often meant groups of barely supervised individuals travelling across the countryside to the appointed place of muster – and trouble and unruly behaviour was all too common. What is really fascinating about this inscription is the fact that it states that a muster was held in Lidgate itself. Musters were usually held in local administrative centres, or at sites that were considered strategically important, not in tiny little Suffolk villages. However, the church at Lidgate is actually built in the outer bailey to a medieval motte-and-bailey castle, whose origins are far from clear but whose earthworks still stand imposingly above the settlement looking out across the village green and duck pond.

While the castle had fallen into decay many centuries before the Armada threat, and would have hardly been considered strategically important, the fact that a muster was held there at all rather suggests that there was at least some residual folk memory of a time when the village had been a centre for military activity.

Military activity actually becomes a strong theme in post-Reformation church graffiti across the country, and most particularly from the time of the English Civil War. Not only was this a time of tremendous local upheaval, with troops being sent many miles from their home counties for long periods of time, but it was also a time when local churches often found themselves stuck fairly and squarely in the front line. The wars were not just between political opponents, but between those of very different religious ideologies. Among the ranks of Cromwell's New Model Army could be found many of those who believed that they had a duty to 'cleanse' the churches of England of what they perceived as 'popery' – in essence, the medieval stained glass, wall paintings, rood screens and other decoration that had survived the onslaught of the Reformation of the previous century. This they did with a vengeance, particularly in Parliamentarian East Anglia, with the troopers supposedly carving their names into the stonework of many a village church. These Puritan sentiments are still to be found etched into many of our churches, such as at Litlington in Cambridgeshire, where the popular Roundhead slogan 'The Pope is Antichrist' is to be seen etched into the surrounding stonework of the priest's door. However, the churches of England were also put to a number of other uses during the Civil War, including being used as temporary prisons for captured enemy soldiers. Among the many graffiti inscriptions to be found in the abbey at St Albans are those reputed to have been made by Royalist prisoners, including one dated 1643, made by 'John Lewis, Soldier'. St Boniface's church, Bunbury in Cheshire, also claims that the many mid-seventeenth-century graffiti inscriptions carved into the magnificent medieval tomb of Sir Hugh de Calveley were done by Civil War prisoners, although local tradition is a little unclear as to which army the troops were meant to have come from.

However, at Burford church in Oxfordshire, it is recorded that there were more than 300 prisoners kept in the church, all of whom had been imprisoned as Leveller mutineers by their own general – no less a person than Oliver Cromwell. The men, sick of war and the long struggle and broken promises of their leaders, had reportedly refused to follow orders and take up arms against the Irish. Oliver Cromwell himself, so local legend states, led a daring night raid into the town and captured the mutineers unawares, locking them in the church under guard. Many of the Leveller prisoners, unsure of their fate, left their names inscribed into the church. Cut deep into the fabric of the font is the almost tangibly bitter inscription: 'Anthony Sedley – 1649 – prisner'. Sedley, however, survived, unlike others of his fellow prisoners. After three days, the ringleaders of the trouble, Coronet Thompson, Corporal Perkins and Private Church, were taken out to the churchyard and executed, Sedley and his fellow prisoners being forced up on to the church roof to watch the spectacle.

Graffiti, of course, didn't stop with the end of the Civil War. Indeed, it can be said to have continued almost unabated right the way through until the nineteenth century, after which point it tends to diminish. It can only be assumed that it is at this period, under Queen Victoria, that the concept of actually carving your name, initials or dates into the stones of the local church becomes seen as something rather anti-social and destructive. The Georgians, however, had no such scruples. You need only walk into any parish church that contains a medieval alabaster tomb to realise that the Georgians believed in making their mark, and leaving it for everyone to see. Some of our finest medieval tombs, such as the effigies of Sir William Lovell at Minster Lovell, Sir William Wilcote at nearby North Leigh, both in Oxfordshire, or that of the Thorpe family at Ashwellthorpe in Norfolk, are quite literally covered with names, dates and initials. Many of these inscriptions are deeply and neatly cut, looking almost as though they had been created by professional stone carvers, and are likely to commemorate visits by these individuals to the church. These early tourists appear to have had no qualms about such high-profile defacement of works of art. Indeed, not even the most prestigious places of worship, or the most important artefacts of England escaped their attention. Westminster Abbey, the site of numerous royal events and the burial place of some of the most notable names in English history, also has its fair share of graffiti. The ancient throne upon which monarchs are actually crowned, known as the Coronation Chair, is deeply covered in eighteenth- and nineteenth-century graffiti. Although this mass of inscriptions was until recently thought to be the work of the schoolchildren from Westminster School, more recent studies suggest that the majority were created by visitors to the abbey – all determined to leave their mark. Little escaped their attention, with deep inscriptions also found on the actual wooden funeral shield of King Edward III, which used to be displayed next to the Coronation Chair.

One of the most common areas to discover more modern graffiti within a church is usually within the bell tower. The ringing chambers of churches, from where the bell ringers actually pull on the bell ropes, are often found to contain numerous examples of later graffiti, many of which appear to have been done by the ringers themselves. Some of these inscriptions refer to the ringing of the bells, often being long columns of numbers running down the walls that recorded 'ringing the changes', as can still be seen on the walls of Troston church in Suffolk. At the church of St Vedast-alias-Foster in the City of London, the ringers took to memorialising themselves on the walls, inscribing their own initials and dates, some of which go back as far as the early eighteenth century. At Pangbourne church in Berkshire, those people who had access to the tower appear to have taken a wider view of the outside world than the ringers of St Vedast. Here, most of the inscriptions are to be found etched into the door and casing of the church clock, and record such diverse events as ice skating on the Thames in 1890 and RAF raids upon the German city of Dusseldorf in 1942. It appears that it wasn't just the local bell ringers who felt the need to leave inscriptions in the bell tower, either. Redenhall church, on the Norfolk and Suffolk border, has long been recognised for its excellent quality of bells and, as a result, teams of bell ringers have visited the church since as far back as the late eighteenth century. In most cases, they appear to have left graffiti of their visit in the tower, most usually just their name or initials, date of the visit and place of origin. However, a few have felt the need to leave more enlightening comments. One critical nineteenth-century inscription on the woodwork asks the question, 'Is the dead and rotten old protestant worship, consisting of a read duet between Parson and Clerk entitled to the least respect?' Below which, in a different hand, is to be found the answer 'NO.'

However, even these late inscriptions in the bell towers of our churches do have a solid and recognisable historic value. At Litcham church in

Norfolk, the ringing chamber of the tower is absolutely covered in graffiti inscriptions. The inscriptions are so numerous that they now cover the area from floor level up to almost three metres, indicating that ladders must have been used in their creation. So many are they that they have even spread out from the walls into the window reveals. Dating back as far as the early eighteenth century, some of the inscriptions appear to be of the names of the bell ringers themselves, and their leader, or tower captain, all enclosed within a highly decorative border. However, the more intriguing inscriptions are those of couples, all accompanied by a date and often set within decorative outlines of a stylised church building. Indeed, it would appear that the bell ringers of Litcham, for whatever reason, left the names of the couples for all of the weddings that they were called to ring for. The result is a unique record of parish weddings etched across the wall of the church tower.

The other group of individuals who are renowned for leaving their mark upon churches are the craftsmen who work on them. Like the medieval mason at Ashwell, Hertfordshire, who commented on the stonework that 'the corners are not joined correctly – I spit on you', builders and craftsmen in more recent centuries have also left a record of their work etched into the very fabric of the church itself. The most obvious of these markings tend to be those left by the 'plumbers' or lead workers. With church roofs commonly made entirely of lead, they are in need of a great deal of maintenance and, every few centuries, major replacements. For the large-scale replacements, the plumbers often cast special plaques, emblazoned with their name and the date of the works, and numerous examples of these can be seen throughout the country. At Appleby Magna in Leicestershire, an extensive restoration of the roof in 1980 led to the removal of several plumbers' plaques that had been in place since the last major roof repairs in 1829. These plaques not only included the name of the plumber and the date, but also the details of the-then rector and the two churchwardens who oversaw the work. Although removed from the roof, the church had the good sense to preserve the plaques, which are still on view in the south aisle.

Alongside the plumbers, the other group of craftsmen likely to have left graffiti inscriptions in the church they were working on are the glaziers. Their inscriptions are to be found on glass in churches all over the country, from the very elaborate to the simple scratched name and date. Alongside the simple messages from the glaziers, such as that found in the church porch at Redenhall, Norfolk, glass graffiti can also be as diverse as any traditional graffiti inscription. At Tilney St Lawrence, in the heart of the bleak Fens landscape of western East Anglia, the glaziers' graffiti has been joined by those of visitors to this magnificent church, with some inscriptions dating back to the early nineteenth century. At the church of St Martin-cum-Gregory in York, one small pane of glass has a beautifully etched, politically motivated inscription that refers to the Battle of Culloden in the eighteenth century. Graffiti on glass is actually likely to be far more common than we currently believe to be the case. Very little analysis has been made on the subject and the fact that they are so difficult to see, particularly on bright sunny days, means that it is all too easy to walk past dozens of examples without ever realising they are there. Throughout history, builders and craftsmen have also used the walls of churches as convenient places in which to work out their accounts. Back at Ashwell church, there is a medieval inscription in the tower of a double column of figures, which appears to be the wages sheet for those employed in the tower's construction. Created over four centuries later, an almost identical inscription can be found on the walls of Cley church in Norfolk. Exactly what work the accounts relate to is unknown, but what is certain is that the maths leaves a great deal to be desired; perhaps unsurprisingly, though, the accounts mistakes all tend to favour one side.

The one area in which post-Reformation graffiti does appear to echo those examples from the medieval period is in memorial inscriptions. Long after the walls of our churches have stopped being etched with magical symbols and marks to ward off the evil eye and any passing demons, they continue to be used to record the passing of individual members of the congregation. While the upper classes might have elaborate wall-mounted monuments of marble and alabaster, the poorer folk were left, as ever, to leave their message scratched into the walls themselves. At Stansfield church in Suffolk, a neatly and deeply cut inscription that partially wraps itself around one of the pillars states that, 'J F Died the forst day of februray 1708.' Although, today, we have no idea exactly who 'J F' was, it would undoubtedly have been enough to identify him to his fellow churchgoers. A few miles away at Lidgate church is a tiny and neat inscription located just inside the tower doorway. Executed in a lovely copperplate hand, it reads simply, 'J. L. Wiseman, departed this life, June 15th 1811.' Although a relatively recent inscription, we can not be sure as to exactly who J. L. Wiseman was; and as no stone appears to his name in the graveyard, it must be assumed he was too poor to have one created. Like so many of those who had gone before him, like the centuries of commoners who had lived, loved and died in this quiet Suffolk parish, this faint and difficult-to-make-out inscription may be the only mark that the life of J. L. Wiseman has left upon this world.

POSTSCRIPT

Stylised bird graffiti, Parham, Suffolk

'All ye who stop to read this stone
Consider how soon she was gone.
Death does not always warning give
Therefore be careful how you live'

The grave of Mary Richards,
died June 1771, aged 31, Doddington, Cambridgeshire

So what can the investigation into medieval graffiti really tell us about the medieval church and how our ancestors interacted with it? How is it changing our perceptions of the past? Well, for the answer to those questions, we must return to Blakeney church, sitting proudly on the north Norfolk coast, and its fleet of little graffiti ships that sail along the piers of the south arcade. As we have seen, all of those little ships, in common with other medieval-graffiti inscriptions, would have been far, far more visible at the time they were made than they are today. Nowadays, all but the very deepest are invisible except with the use of specialist lighting, and anyone who has ever wandered through a medieval church or two has quite probably passed many dozens by without even realising they were there. In fact, this relative invisibility is quite probably what has protected the inscriptions from the attentions of overenthusiastic restorers for all these centuries. Had they been more obvious, then, in all likelihood, the dead hand of Victorian over-restoration would have done away with them in an instant. However, as already mentioned with regard to ship graffiti, at the time most of these inscriptions were made, the church interior looked very different from the way most churches look today. Most would have been a riot of colour and pigment, with the graffiti cut through the paintwork to reveal the white stone beneath. As a result, the graffiti inscriptions, far from being hidden away in dark corners and difficult to see, would have been one of the most obvious things you saw upon entering the church. Certainly, the upper sections of the walls would have been the battleground of painted angels, demons and saints – and the windows a translucent jumble of colour – but the wall right in front of you, at eye level, was covered in small white images standing out against the colour-washed background.

In the case of Blakeney church, this means that the pier in the south arcade that is covered in ship graffiti, which we know from surviving pigment fragments was painted a deep red colour, would actually have looked like a fleet of little white ships sailing across a deep red ocean.

We also know that those ships were created over a two- to three-hundred-year period; and that the earlier ones were still clearly visible when the later ones were created as they all respect the space of those around them, and don't normally cross over each other. Now here is the thing. At just about any point in that two- to three-hundred-year period, the rector, vicar or churchwardens could have defaced those inscriptions; they could have scraped them from the walls or covered them with more paintwork. However, they didn't. We know this because two hundred years after the first inscriptions were made, they were still visible, and those creating the later inscriptions could avoid crossing over them. What, then, can this tell us about the attitudes at the time towards these graffiti inscriptions?

This lack of defacement by the church authorities on a local level rather suggests that these inscriptions were both accepted and acceptable within the medieval parish. They were seen for exactly what they really were. Not something destructive and anti-social, to be discouraged and frowned upon, but as something with both spiritual meaning and devotional function. They were simply the lasting physical manifestation of prayers; prayers made solid in stone.

From this, it becomes clear that the medieval church was a far more interactive space than we may once have believed. It was far more than just a building that you entered to view the parish priest undertake the rituals and traditions of the church; to see the miraculous elevation of the Host. It was far more than just a canvas onto which the pretty pigments of the wall paintings were applied; and a stone framework into which the glittering wonders of the coloured-glass windows were set. It was a building that you were meant and required to interact with on a number of different levels, and one of the most fundamental of those levels was the physical. The medieval parish church was, and remains today, far more than just a gallery of lost glories; it is the stone, lead and plaster canvas upon which generations of people inscribed their faith. Perhaps the most amazing thing of all is that all those testaments of faith and devotion, etched into the stones by countless generations of worshippers, are still there for all to see – the lost voices of the medieval church.

GLOSSARY

Typical example of the 'Holy Monogram', Framlingham, Suffolk

Aisle: the parts of a church to the north and south of the nave, most usually built as extensions to accommodate larger congregations. Often home to aisle altars.

Aisle altar: besides the main altar, or high altar, churches often contained smaller altars at the east end of the north and south aisles. Traditionally, the altar on the north side was dedicated to the Virgin Mary and known as the Mary altar. The south altar was often dedicated to the church's patron saint.

Apotropaic: from the Greek *apotropaios*, meaning literally 'to ward off'. Apotropaic markings and symbols were used to ward off evil and protect individuals and localities from malign influence. Such markings are often known as ritual protection marks or witch marks.

Ambulatory: most usually only found in larger churches and cathedrals, an ambulatory is an area specifically designed to walk in, or for processions to pass through. This could refer in some cases to the cloister, but most usually refers to a walkway found around the eastern end of the building.

Arcade: a row of arches supported by piers, usually between the nave and the aisle.

Bar tracery: introduced into England in the middle of the thirteenth century, bar tracery superseded plate tracery. With bar tracery, the stone ribs and vaults were designed to be structural and support the weight of the wall into which they were inserted. The introduction of bar tracery thereby allowed the creation of far larger windows than had previously been possible, without weakening the structure.

Black Death: see bubonic plague.

Brasses: these are inscribed memorial tablets of copper alloy, most usually set within the floor of a church. They often show portraits of the deceased with an inscription noting their name and date of death. The earliest brasses in England date to the second half of the thirteenth century, the fashion continuing until the middle decades of the seventeenth century.

Bubonic plague: often referred to as the Black Death, but at the time known usually as the 'pestilence', this disease first spread to England in 1348 and within twelve months had killed approximately a third of the population. After this, the plague was a regular visitor to these shores, culminating in the Great Plague of London in 1665. It is thought that the disease was spread by fleas that passed the disease by biting the victims. Although often fatal, there were numerous cases of individuals actually recovering from the disease. An airborne variant of the disease, known as pneumonic plague, was almost always fatal.

Candle beam: a horizontal beam running across the chancel arch to which candles or lights were fixed. Sometimes formed part of the rood screen. Accessed via the rood stair.

Chancel: the section of the church at the east end, traditionally separated from the nave by the rood screen. The chancel was where the main altar was located. Access to the chancel was usually restricted to the parish priest and those celebrating Mass. Legal and financial responsibility for the chancel was often with the priest or rector, while the nave fell to the parish.

Chantry: a chantry chapel was established by an individual, or group of well-off individuals, to ensure that prayers for their soul continued after death, thereby reducing the amount of time they would spend in purgatory. Upon occasion, the donor or patron was buried within the chapel itself, and priests were employed to ensure the flow of continual prayers for the benefactor's soul. At the other end of the spectrum, the term chantry was given to any long-term bequest that sought to establish a routine or prayers for the soul of the donor. Chantry bequests could last for as little as a month after the donor's death, or sometimes continue for several generations.

Clerestory: an upper level or storey above the nave, most usually pierced with windows allowing extra light into the central area of the church.

Cloister: from the Latin *claustrum*, meaning an enclosed space, is most usually found only in the larger religious houses and cathedrals. It is formed of covered walkways set around a rectangular open space known as the cloister garth. Cloisters are usually set upon the warmer south side of the building and were used as areas of both recreation and work.

Cog: a single-masted square-rigged sailing vessel that was commonly used from the twelfth century onwards and would have been a common site in English ports. Often depicted with a prominent raised bow, giving it a distinctive and easily identifiable profile.

Consecration cross: most usually, a painted or inscribed cross located on the walls of the church. By tradition, the bishop would anoint a newly built church twelve times inside and twelve times outside with holy oil when the building was first consecrated. The places where the oil was applied to the walls were then marked with a cross. Many English churches still contain examples of surviving medieval consecration crosses.

Corbel: a supporting plinth set into a wall to carry weight of a structure above, such as a timber roof or stone vaulting. Corbels were often highly decorated and carved into images of heads or grotesques.

Flint flushwork: a decorative technique commonly used on late medieval churches, where knapped flints are set flush within a stone or brick border to create a two-tone pattern.

Guild: there are two main types of medieval guild trade (craft) guilds and religious guilds. Trade guilds were established to regulate a craft trade within a particular locality, and controlled everything from the hiring of apprentices to quality control and pricing. Most trade guilds also undertook religious and social duties such as maintaining a light in a local church, looking after members who became ill and ensuring prayers for the souls of departed members. Religious guilds were established along the same lines, but without the requirement of being involved in a particular craft organisation to join them. The wealthy guilds often had dedicated altars within churches for which they took financial responsibility.

Heraldry: the formalised identification of families and individuals by the use of specific devices and motifs. Traditionally thought to have developed in the eleventh and twelfth centuries as a method of identifying individuals amid the chaos of a battlefield from the device on their shields.

IHS: known as the Sacred Monogram, but with no clear and undisputed origin. Some believe it to be the initial letters of *Iesus Hominum Salvator* (Jesus, the saviour of mankind), while others believe it to be taken from the Greek spelling of the name of Jesus. Whatever its origins, it turns up in all forms of church decoration and is a common graffiti motif.

Knights Templar: a religious and military order formed in 1119 with the express purpose of protecting pilgrims travelling to the Holy Land. Their military success soon lead to wealth and political power and the establishment of a Europe-wide administrative system far beyond any government of the day. However, the order and its reputed wealth also attracted enemies, culminating in a plot between King Philip of France and Pope Clement V to bring their downfall. The order was officially disbanded in 1312.

Lady chapel: a chapel dedicated to the Virgin Mary, often found in larger churches or cathedrals, and most usually located on the north side of the church. The growth of the cult of the Virgin Mary in the later Middle Ages was reflected in an increase in the popularity of Lady chapels and Marian imagery in general. Sometimes also known as a Mary chapel.

Ledger stone: inscribed or incised stone memorial slab set into the floor of the church. Often made of expensive marbles, these slabs are sometimes elaborately decorated with coats of arms and portraits, as well as the more usual text inscriptions.

Mary/Marian Altar: in churches that had no separate Lady chapel, the altar at the east end of the north aisle, if present, was often dedicated to the Virgin Mary. The north side of the church was the traditional side for the female parishioners to be and Mary altars often became the focus for bequests and gifts from the women of the parish.

Mason's mark: incised marks created by medieval masons to identify the areas of the building that they had worked upon. Used as both an administrative tool, allowing the master mason to calculate the wages due to each mason, and as a quality-control mark.

Mass dial: an incised decoration that takes the form of a small sundial and often found located on the south side of churches, near the porch or priest's door. Consists of a central hole with lines radiating out from it, traditionally thought to indicate the times of services.

Master mason: the role of the medieval master mason was one of architect, technical director and clerk of works. As well as designing the building, master masons were often contracted to oversee construction and supervise the everyday activities of the workforce. However, by the later Middle Ages, the role was often seen as one of designer and consultant, and building contracts were forced to include clauses expressly forbidding a master mason from leaving one unfinished job to undertake new works elsewhere.

Merchant's mark: each merchant would have their own individual mark that they used to mark their goods, sign documents and adorn their property. They were, in essence, the logo of the Middle Ages and were designed to be easily recognisable to both the literate and illiterate. Merchant's marks have been described as being the heraldry of the medieval merchant classes.

Misericords: from the Latin *misericordia*, meaning to have mercy upon, and referring to the small ledge located beneath the tip-up seats in choir stalls. These ledges were to allow the elderly and infirm to rest themselves during long services and were often decorated with strange cravings and reliefs.

Mullion: a vertical shaft in a window dividing one area from another.

Nave: from the Latin *navis*, meaning ship, and referring to the main or central part of the church where the congregation would be during services. The nave was the parish's part of the church and they were most usually responsible for its repair and upkeep.

Niche image: a small recess within a wall, against a pier or on the outside of a building into which a devotional statue was placed. Often surrounded by a decorative canopy and originally painted and gilded. Image niches often became the centre for small devotional cults aimed at particular saints and points of concentration for graffiti inscriptions.

Parclose: a screen designed to separate the main body of the church from the north or south aisle, most usually to create an enclosed space for a side chapel or chantry chapel.

Patron saint: the saint to whom a church was dedicated. In some cases this saint could alter over the centuries and the church dedication could change, leading to an amusing amount of confusion among historians.

Pier: the architectural term used to describe a pillar or column within the church.

Pillar: see pier.

Plate tracery: an early form of window tracery that essentially involved building a wall and then cutting a window opening in it, thereby limiting the size of window that could be created without causing the wall to collapse.

Quoins: the stones on the outside corners and angles of the church, such as buttresses.

Rebus: a puzzle, often a mixture of letters, words and images designed to represent a name, phrase or saying. More complex examples of rebus inscriptions, such as those found at Lidgate church in Suffolk, are formed of a mixture of letters, musical notation and images.

Reformation: the name referring to the period in the middle of the sixteenth century that saw the break from the authority of the Church of Rome and the gradual development of a Protestant church within

England. The exact dates of the Reformation and its extent are still the subject of debate among scholars. However, in most general terms the Reformation is considered to have begun in 1534 with the Act of Supremacy, which declared that Henry VIII was the Supreme Head of the Church of England.

Ringing chamber: a chamber within the tower from which the bells are rung. In some cases, this can be within the base of the tower, in others it is a specially formed chamber on a higher level.

Ritual protection mark: see Apotropaic.

Rood: from the Anglo-Saxon, meaning cross, the rood was the large image of the crucifixion located above the rood screen in the chancel arch.

Rood screen: a screen that separates the nave from the chancel. The lower section usually has panels that contain images of the saints, while the upper section tends to be tracery-style work. Above this was set a canopy or gallery and candle beam. The upper sections were accessed via a rood-loft stair, which was located within the thickness of the church wall. The whole was surmounted by the rood.

Scratch dial: see Mass dial.

Spandrels: the triangular area formed between the upper areas of an arch and the horizontal and vertical surrounds. Often highly decorated.

Sweating sickness: a disease that is first recorded in England in 1485 and may well have been imported by the foreign mercenaries brought to England to support Henry Tudor. The disease was both deadly and fast-acting, with victims traditionally being talked of as 'well at dinner time and dead by supper'. The exact nature of the disease is still unknown, although it is now thought that a type of hantavirus appears the most likely cause. The disease reputedly only broke out during the reigns of the male Tudor monarchs.

Tracery, window: the decorative stonework that fills the upper sections of window spaces, supported by mullions. See also, bar tracery and plate tracery.

Transepts: in a cruciform-shaped church or cathedral, the projecting wings to north and south.

Tympanum: the decorated space above a door head.

Witch mark: see apotropaic.

SELECTED SITES TO VISIT

Listed below is a small selection of sites to visit that contain good examples of early graffiti inscriptions. In most cases, these churches and castles are open daily and welcome visitors. However, remember that most of these sites are still active places of worship continuing a centuries' long tradition – so please be respectful. Keeping these sites in good repair and open to the public takes not only a great deal of dedication from the various rectors, vicars and churchwardens, but also a good deal of money as well. Therefore, if you do visit and enjoy hunting for the graffiti, please don't be afraid to leave a small donation to the church. Lastly, most of these churches usually have a visitors' book; try to take a few minutes to record your visit. The knowledge that others have visited, admired and enjoyed their own little piece of English medieval history does mean a very great deal to those local people who daily strive to keep these amazing buildings in good order. The work is often hard, the hours long and the thanks are few and far between.

This short list represents only a tiny number of the sites where early graffiti has been recorded, and there are still many hundreds of churches out there that have yet to be fully surveyed. While there are amazing inscriptions to be seen at these sites, it is just as likely that there are still many other wonderful and important examples still out there awaiting discovery. Some perhaps just around the corner, simply waiting for someone to turn up with a torch . . .

BEDFORDSHIRE

Leighton Buzzard All Saints is, whichever way you look at it, a truly magnificent church. The massive stone spire and intricate tracery of the east end make it a place of pilgrimage for medievalists and architectural historians from all around the country, particularly given that it was only a few short decades ago that we came close to losing the whole church in a fire. Luckily, most of the wonderful graffiti in the church survived the fire virtually unscathed. The church contains a fine depiction of a late-medieval soldier, medieval text, crowns, heraldry and two very elaborate pieces of architectural graffiti, as well as the usual bevy of animals, birds and witch marks.

Shillington The graffiti in the church at Shillington was first brought to the public's attention by historian Violet Pritchard in the 1960s. She recognised the site as being important not only for the quantity of graffiti present, but also because of the quality and diversity of the inscriptions. The church contains good examples of many of the main types of medieval graffiti including pentangles, knights' heads, heraldic inscriptions, musical instruments and a good selection of general witch marks. The church itself is hard to miss, built on a chalky outcrop that dominates the surrounding countryside. The poet John Betjeman described it as 'the Cathedral of the Chilterns'. Who are we to argue?

CAMBRIDGESHIRE

Ely Cathedral In terms of graffiti, the main body of the Cathedral is too early, with too rough a stone, to contain any great collection, but there are nice examples in the Lady chapel that are well worth a look. However, the real hidden graffiti treasure of the cathedral can be found on your way in. On the walls of the western porch, known as a 'Galilee Porch', are some of the most complete and fascinating medieval architectural drawings to be found anywhere in England. Dating to the middle of the thirteenth century, they represent the working drawings of the medieval master mason as he played with fresh ideas and new designs that helped form England's Gothic revolution.

Kingston The church is perhaps best known for its rather important surviving medieval wall paintings that date from the thirteenth century all the way through to the sixteenth or seventeenth century. The paintings themselves show a huge variety of scenes, including two very spectacular lance-wielding knights, the seven works of mercy, demons, devils and the remains of a large St Christopher. The other notable feature of the church is the very soft chalk-like material that has been used to build the pillars of the arcades. The softness of the material makes carving graffiti into the surface really quite simple, and it would appear that many generations of locals have taken advantage of this.

Sawston A truly well-loved church with a busy and welcoming congregation who are enthusiastic about all aspects of their beautiful building, including its many graffiti inscriptions. A quick look at the chancel arch will reveal that Sawston church not only has a good collection of ritual-protection marks – it actually has the full set! In one small area on the east face of the arch, there can be seen compass-drawn designs, pentangles, pelta patterns and 'VV' symbols, all crowded onto a small area of the stonework. Elsewhere in the church can be found requests for prayers, Latin mottos and further, very elaborate compass-drawn designs.

Westley Waterless While the outside of the church may be a little uninspiring, the interior is full of wonderful little survivals. The font is a medieval delight, with each face carved in a different pattern, and, nearby, can be seen a selection of grave slabs said to have been created for members of the Order of Knights Templar. In terms of early graffiti, the church has a fine selection, even if some examples are in less-than-perfect condition. There are all the usual witch marks and compass-drawn designs, and a good amount of early text, too. However, the finest inscription is a long piece of early-Latin text that Violet Pritchard believed referred to the growing of grapes for the production of communion wine, perhaps even in the churchyard!

CUMBRIA

Carlisle Cathedral A little bigger than the average parish church but not as big as you might expect, particularly since the Civil Wars of the seventeenth century when Scottish soldiers quarried part of the west end for stone to reinforce Carlisle Castle. The building probably contains less graffiti than many cathedrals, perhaps the result of the slightly rough feel of the stone itself, but it does boast a veritable wealth of medieval mason's marks. However, the real graffiti gems here are the two extremely rare runic inscriptions – only one of which is generally accessible to the public (and is to be found very near the main entrance). While in Carlisle it is worth taking the time to look at the castle as well, for here too you will find a mass of early graffiti spread around the keep. The real stars of the show are to be seen in the area around the medieval chapel, now behind a glass door, where deeply cut inscriptions show saints, animals and armed men.

Lanercost Priory The priory itself is split in two, with the ruins of most of the complex being in the care of English Heritage (entrance fees apply), while most of the original priory church was taken on by the community at the time of the Reformation, and now acts as the parish church. The English Heritage part of the site is well worth a look; there are really nice examples of mason's marks and medieval board games cut into the stones, as well as some intriguing reused Roman material from nearby Hadrian's Wall. There is also a lovely old 'Ministry of Works' sign that reminds visitors that they will face prosecution if they are found adding graffiti to the stones. However, once inside the priory church, you soon realise that the sign was clearly erected several centuries too late. The walls of the church contain many examples of medieval text, mason's marks and ritual protection marks that shed light on the human story of this lovely building and its sometimes turbulent border history.

ESSEX

Belchamp Walter For many people, the church at Belchamp Walter might be what they consider the archetypal East Anglian parish church. The church has some superb surviving wall paintings, but also holds other treasures, most notably a fine collection of early graffiti. There is a good selection of witch marks to be seen as well as birds, animals and a good amount of medieval text – the most notable of which is slightly hidden away on the door to the tower. Here, you can find a long list of names, dated to the sixteenth century from the style of lettering, and, apparently, a list of locals, which includes the vicar and, most probably, the churchwardens, including Henry Man, John Gylet and John Coomb.

Great Bardfield The inside of the church is a little bit on the ornate side for some tastes, set off with a bright mixture of coloured glass, but there is no denying the sheer elegance and pure quality of the pillars and window tracery. It's a church that reeks of ancient money spent by noble patrons for the glory of God – and perhaps also their own reputations. There isn't a great deal of early graffiti at Great Bardfield, but what is there is of extremely good quality. The most obvious are several late-medieval text inscriptions, some of which have yet to be transcribed, and an elegant medieval rebus inscription – much like that found at Lidgate church over the border in Suffolk.

Steeple Bumpstead The most obvious thing you will notice upon arrival at Steeple Bumpstead church is that there isn't one. A steeple that is. If there ever was a steeple, and even that is open to question despite many folk tales, then it was gone by the sixteenth century when large parts of the upper section of the tower were rebuilt in brick. The graffiti in the church is diverse and important, with good examples of dated medieval inscription, most probably referring to the arrival of the plague in the village. Alongside these inscriptions is a fine collection of medieval images, including knights in mail armour, animals, geometric designs and many other examples of early text. Steeple or no steeple, it is well worth a look.

GLOUCESTERSHIRE

Churchdown St Bartholomew's is a church that's difficult to miss for a good number of reasons. First, its built right on top of a hill (Chosen

Hill) that appears to be at least partly man-made, and the whole is surrounded by the ramparts of an Iron Age hillfort. Local tradition has it that this was a sacred site long before the church was built here and most probably long before the coming of Christianity to this remote part of the country. The graffiti here is mainly located in the porch and consists of some real rarities, including a head of Christ, the only known mermaid inscription in England and what appears to be a spouting whale. Well worth the long climb uphill.

HERTFORDSHIRE

Anstey The church of St George is an unusual one in many ways. The most obvious point to notice is that it is built in a cruciform shape, with a central tower, giving the odd impression that the whole building is bigger than it actually is. The graffiti inside the church is also rather special, with a fantastic collection of inscriptions that include numerous shields and coats of arms, crested helmets and heraldic beasts. The wealth of military imagery has been suggested to stem from the fact that the church was built in close association with nearby Anstey Castle – a motte-and-bailey earthwork originally built in the twelfth century by Eustace, Count of Boulogne.

Ashwell Of all churches containing medieval graffiti, and it does contain rather a lot of inscriptions, Ashwell is probably the best studied. It has been explored by scholars, examined by historians, peered at by archae-ologists, and I even popped in a couple of times, too. Despite this, the truly amazing thing about the graffiti at Ashwell, particularly the unusu-ally large number of medieval text inscriptions, is that even after all this study and research nobody can quite agree as to exactly what many of the inscriptions say – let alone what they might mean. The church is famous for the inscriptions in the tower, one that refers to the arrival of the plague in the village, and a depiction of old St Paul's Cathedral, which was destroyed in the Great Fire of London. However, the rest of the church is also well covered in medieval text inscriptions.

St Albans The abbey church is one of the few very large medieval buildings in England that has been seriously surveyed for early graffiti inscriptions, and with some exciting results. Some of the graffiti is now highlighted in a short guidebook published by the Friends of St Albans Abbey, which takes the form of a fascinating and enlightening short tour of the building. Across the walls can be found animals and birds, medieval figures, allegorical scenes and a good selection of medieval text. Among my own personal favourites are a charming image of a small cat that appears to be curled up as though asleep, a beautiful arch-necked swan and an elegant piece of medieval script claimed to be the signature of 'Syr John Mandevyll knight'.

KENT

Canterbury Cathedral As one of the largest, finest and oldest cathedrals in England, Canterbury Cathedral is full of early graffiti. I would advise any visitor to take their time exploring this remarkable building, beginning with the cloisters.

St Margarets-at-Cliffe The church at St Margarets-at-Cliffe is a little unusual in the fact that Victorian restoration here didn't actually destroy the graffiti, but rather brought it to light. Between 1864 and 1867, the massive stone piers of the church were cleaned of their many layers of post-Reformation limewash, revealing a mass of medieval text, ships and other markings that had been hidden for centuries, and quickly became the subject of study by historians and antiquarians. While in the vicinity of Dover, there are two other places that are definitely worth a visit by anyone interested in graffiti. The first is Dover Castle, now in the care of English Heritage (admission charges apply), which, like many English castles, is also crammed full of graffiti inscriptions. The second, which sits just down the hill from the castle entrance, is a little more unusual. The White Horse Inn, which dates back to the Middle Ages, has begun a whole new graffiti tradition over the last few decades; anyone who has successfully managed to swim the English Channel is encouraged to sign their name on the walls and ceiling of the public bar. Today, it is covered with a mass of graffiti inscriptions, with everyone from charity swimmers to world-record holders having made their mark. It's certainly a unique historical record!

Westerham The church has some lovely examples of graffiti dotted around, including an elaborate compass-drawn design on the tower arch and a mass of sixteenth- and seventeenth-century inscriptions towards the chancel. A recent survey of the church even noted the inscribed outlines of medieval consecration crosses high up on the pillars, which had gone unnoticed for centuries. My personal favourite is an elegant monogram design of the initials 'J B' dated to 1595 – the year William Shakespeare is believed to have written *A Midsummer Night's Dream*.

LEICESTERSHIRE

Croxton Kerrial The church was originally dedicated to St Botolph. However, at some point in the dim and distant past (most probably the sixteenth century), the dedication was changed to St John the Baptist instead, which it remains to this day; baffling documentary historians as they plough through the parish history looking for the 'lost' church. However, the real place to look for medieval text is the walls of the church themselves. Croxton Kerrial contains a mass of graffiti inscriptions, including a great deal of medieval text that nobody has yet transcribed, as well as medieval soldiers, heraldic devices and all the usual collection of witch marks and ritual protection marks.

LINCOLNSHIRE

Bassingham When Violet Pritchard published her book on English Medieval Graffiti in 1967, she featured an inscription that showed an early-sixteenth-century ship. The vessel was really quite superb, with rigging, gun ports and even decoration shown on the hull, and it was to be found, according to the book, at Marton church, a dozen or so miles north-west of Lincoln. So good was the depiction of the ship that lots of people including a good number of maritime historians went looking for it. However, no matter how hard they looked, no matter which dark corners they peered their torches into, they simply could not find it. Rumours of its destruction abounded.

However, the truth was rather simpler. When Pritchard did her surveys, she relied upon making rubbings of the graffiti on loose sheets of paper, and just occasionally they got muddled up and put in the wrong file. Therefore, if you do really want to see one of the finest pieces of ship graffiti in England, it is to Bassingham, not Marton, you must go.

Bassingthorpe Although none of the graffiti at Bassingthorpe can really be considered outstanding, it does have a really lovely cross section of just about everything. There are ships, there are shoe inscriptions, there are faces and there are lots of lovely compass-drawn designs, too. Witch marks are to be found all over the place and, if you look carefully, you will even find the remains of the odd medieval gaming board. However, what really stands out at Bassingthorpe is the number and quality of seventeenth- and eighteenth-century inscriptions. Some of them are, quite simply, beautiful and worth a visit in their own right.

Lincoln Cathedral Most medieval cathedrals are full of early-graffiti inscriptions and Lincoln is certainly no exception. Just about every surface in this building is covered in graffiti dating from the fourteenth and fifteenth centuries right through to almost the present day. And it isn't just the wide date range that makes the graffiti here of interest, but the wide range of subject matter, too. All the medieval 'usual suspects' are present, as are some really rare architectural inscriptions, and the nave piers contain very early examples of dated graffiti that you won't find in too many other places. Many of the inscriptions appear to be concentrated in the area of the crossing, including many of the post-Reformation examples, suggesting that this part of the cathedral has always been a place where people gathered together – much as they still do today.

NORFOLK

The churches of the Glaven Port Five or six hundred years ago, the parishes of Blakeney, Wiveton, Cley-next-the-sea and Salthouse formed one of the busiest sea ports in East Anglia – known collectively as the

Glaven port after the small river upon which it stands. Today, it is difficult to visualise this serene piece of the north Norfolk coast as once having been home to the vast fleets of fishing and merchant vessels that plied their trade from as far away as Greenland and the Baltic. No matter what time of year you visit, you can hardly fail to notice the magnificent churches, all built with the riches of medieval trade and industry. Although the port declined in the later Middle Ages – the result of the gradual silting up of the harbour – the churches still stand as testament to the area's past fortune. Here, you can discover many, many superb examples of early graffiti, including one of the finest collections of medieval ship graffiti to be found anywhere in England. Each church is different, and each is a gem.

Litcham The 'town' of Litcham is set in the centre of Norfolk, built upon an important crossroads that linked the east and west of the county. The church is also relatively modest, having been largely rebuilt in the early fifteenth century, with the unusual brick-built tower having been added in the seventeenth century. The church boasts many treasures, among which the fantastic collection of early graffiti must be considered a highlight. Here, you will find everything from demons and dogs to beautiful compass-drawn designs and prayers etched into the soft pillars of the arcade. One of my favourites.

Ludham A small cathedral of a church in the heart of the Norfolk Broads that boasts a mass of wonderful medieval survivals. Graffiti is to be found all over the church, with a lovely selection of crosses around the south door and elaborate compass-drawn designs on the tower arch. And don't forget to look up. High on a pillar at the west end of the south arcade, you can still make out clear medieval text – the name of the vicar etched into the building during reconstruction works in the early fifteenth century.

Norwich Cathedral Like many other medieval cathedrals, it is full of examples of early graffiti. Over five thousand inscriptions have been recorded in the cathedral, with the earliest believed to date to the twelfth century. There are good examples of just about every major type of graffiti to be found all over the building, from medieval text in the cloisters to superb medieval ships next to the organ. The building has been much altered over the centuries, but these changes too are reflected in the graffiti, leaving a concise record of the life of a medieval cathedral literally etched into the walls.

NORTHAMPTONSHIRE

Ashton An unusual site in the fact that the graffiti isn't actually on the church fabric at all, but on the medieval tomb slabs inside. Many church monuments attract graffiti, much of it relatively recent, but the tombs at Aston have a very fine collection of early graffiti. Alongside heraldic inscriptions can be seen swords, architectural designs and ornate decorative patterns.

Stoke Goldington I'm sure that even the locals will agree that St Peter's church is rather unusual to look at due to the numerous additions and rebuilding it has gone through over the centuries. The church contains some very fine medieval-Latin text inscriptions, some of which still defy full transcription, as well as the usual selection of witch marks and later inscriptions. The walls also contain sketches by some of the medieval masons who built the church, outlining carvings and moulding profiles. A fascinating place.

SUFFOLK

Lidgate If you have a few days to spare, a Thermos flask full of nourishing soup and an endless supply of torch batteries then Lidgate is the church for you. It is quite simply covered in early graffiti. It's unusual in the number of medieval-text inscriptions to be seen, many of which have yet to be fully transcribed, and is well known for its connection to the medieval poet John Lydgate, who may actually have been responsible for some of the inscriptions. As well as the medieval text, there are fantastic examples of medieval windmills, demons and witch marks to be seen all over the building. The church was originally built within the bailey of a now-long-lost castle, and the impressive and well-preserved earthworks can still be seen behind the church.

Parham A simple and beautifully well-kept church that is full of light and hidden delights. Although the church doesn't have a fantastic quantity of graffiti, what is there is rather special. Mainly located on either side of the tower arch, you will find a lovely collection of little medieval ships, musical instruments, text and even the odd medieval face peering back at you from the stonework. What's really unusual at Parham is that much of the graffiti here is relatively easy to date, with most of it originating in the fifteenth century. The graffiti also contains the only depictions so far discovered of a medieval church organ, which would once have filled the space with music.

Troston I have a very soft spot for St Mary's church in Troston. The church's best-known treasure is the simply stunning collection of late-medieval wall paintings that still adorn the walls. However, alongside the wonderful wall paintings, the church also contains a real mass of early-graffiti inscriptions on both the tower arch and chancel arch. Demons are pinned to the walls, medieval ladies raise their hands in prayer, deer and birds are scattered across the stonework and the outline of hands of long-dead parishioners cover the walls of the porch. The graffiti at St Mary's is truly special; a personal glimpse into life in the late-medieval parish.

SURREY

Compton St Nicholas church is believed to date back, in parts, to the eleventh century. Only very small sections of the early fabric survive, and these are hard for the average visitor to spot. The church has a fine collection of early-graffiti inscriptions, among which are many ritual-protection marks, including a lovely compass-drawn motif, many crosses and some very nicely executed early-text inscriptions. Among these text inscriptions appear to be the names John de Brudeford and Gilbert le Mareschal, who have been discovered by local historians in documents dating back to the fourteenth century.

Horley Despite numerous and quite large-scale restorations, St Bartholomew's church has one of the finest collections of early graffiti so far discovered in the county. Alongside the usual collection of witch marks and later inscriptions are some important examples of medieval graffiti. Strange faces wearing outlandish headgear peer back from the walls, while crowns and flowers jostle across the stonework. Most importantly, a long text inscription, one of the few so far discovered in England, declares the church to be the last resting place of Bartholomew Saleman.

Shere Like most Surrey churches, Shere doesn't contain a great mass of early graffiti, most probably because of the significant amount of restoration that has taken place in the past; but what is there is of good quality. Most notably, the church contains far more text inscriptions than you would find in the average church, and a large number of them are clearly medieval in origin. The inscriptions are still neat and crisp – and yet the number of abbreviations and contractions they contain make them a real challenge. They are a mystery that, as yet, awaits unravelling.

SUSSEX

Arundel Formally known as 'The Parish and Priory church of St Nicholas', and largely dating from the late fourteenth century, the building has undergone extensive restoration following storm damage in 2012. However, despite damage to the windows and tower, the graffiti inscriptions, which really are quite special, remained unscathed. The church can boast a really superb collection of early-text inscriptions, most of which appear to be individual names, and many fine examples of compass-drawn motifs. Alongside these are a good number of witch marks, monograms and some very fine post-Reformation graffiti.

Winchelsea The town of New Winchelsea on the south coast was built after the old town, 'Old Winchelsea', was washed away by storms in the thirteenth century. In 1281, Edward I ordered that a new town be planned and built, laid out along a strict grid pattern, with the great church of St Thomas at its centre. The church in particular was planned on a grand, almost cathedral-like scale. Today, all that remains of the church are the massive chancel and east ends of the aisles, and there is some debate as to whether the church was ever fully completed. However, what does remain of the church is packed full of early graffiti and, given the importance of Winchelsea as a medieval port, you will be unsurprised to learn that it has a good collection of ship graffiti, as well as knights, witch marks and heraldic graffiti. Two minutes walk away from the church is Blackfriars barn undercroft, one of over thirty medieval cellars that survive in the town. Now owned by the National Trust (admission charges apply), the undercroft is open to the public on numerous occasions throughout the year and contains one of the most fascinating graffiti scenes in England. All along one wall of the cellar, cut into the plaster when it was still wet, is an entire fleet of medieval ships that appear to date back to the middle of the fourteenth century.

WILTSHIRE

Lacock Abbey The original abbey was founded in the thirteenth century, and dedicated to St Mary and St Bernard. However, the whole site was sold at the time of the Reformation to Sir William Sharington, who pulled down the church and converted the rest of the abbey buildings to a fine Tudor country house. The medieval cloisters are still to be found incorporated into the later house, and here you will find a wealth of graffiti inscriptions from merchant's marks and early ritual-protection marks to early tourist graffiti from the eighteenth and nineteenth centuries. (National Trust property, admission charges apply.)

YORKSHIRE

Beverley Minster Claimed to be the largest parish church in England (an honour also claimed by Hull, Ludlow and Great Yarmouth!), Beverley Minster is actually larger than a third of the cathedrals in England. The shrine of St John of Beverley was a popular destination for medieval pilgrims and his bones are still claimed to lie beneath a plaque in the nave. The minster contains a lovely collection of graffiti, including ships, mason's marks, compass-drawn designs and lots of early text inscriptions.

York Minster The minster actually has far less early graffiti than you might expect from a building of its size and age. This is most probably largely the result of the amount of restoration work that the building has been subjected to after various fires and disasters that it has suffered over the centuries. However, the passage between the north transept and the chapter house, which is lined with benches along both sides, contains a fascinating collection of graffiti inscriptions, including excellent examples of medieval musical notation, mason's marks, board games and medieval text. The presence of things such as the music and board games, particularly those etched into the benches, would seem to suggest that this was an area where members of the community were to be found with a little time on their hands. Many of the other churches in the city also contain good examples of graffiti and are well worth spending some time exploring.

LONDON

Southwark Cathedral When it was first built, and for long centuries afterwards, Southwark Cathedral was the tallest, most imposing structure on London's south bank. Although today dwarfed by almost every building in the vicinity, it still exudes an air of formal grandeur, as any visitor to its lofty interior will soon discover. The cathedral has seen many restorations, which have wiped much early graffiti from the walls, but there is still much to see. Hunt out the oldest parts of the stonework and you will come across mason's marks, strange animals, early text and much more.

ACKNOWLEDGEMENTS

This book would not have been possible without the hard work and enthusiasm of all the volunteers who took part in the graffiti surveys throughout the country. None received anything in return for the hours they spent in sometimes damp and freezing churches, staring at the walls – except friendship, gratitude and the utmost respect from their peers and myself. Every single volunteer is, in my opinion, a star – and each of them can now add 'medieval-graffiti expert' to their respective CVs. In particular, thanks must go to some of the stalwart volunteers, team leaders and county survey leaders – Colin Howey, Paul Judkins, Terry Eglington, Pat May, Brian Porter, Matt Beresford, Nat Cohen, Richard Neville, Hugh Lanham and Emily Watts – and all of the 'special' Norwich Cathedral survey teams who, as a result of my own appalling memory for names, all conveniently renamed themselves. All of them, with no previous archaeological experience, surveyed an entire cathedral that contained over 5,000 individual inscriptions – and they never stopped smiling once.

Thanks are also due to all the rectors, vicars and churchwardens of the hundreds of churches throughout England who not only suffered our intrusions into their churches but actually made us very welcome. They opened doors, allowed us access to hidden-away corners, accompanied us on death-defying ascents of crumbling tower stairs, shared the excitement of making new discoveries – and then gave us all tea and cake. People who suggest that the Church of England is dead or dying need only meet a few dozen of these parish stalwarts to realise that it is, in fact, alive and well. Without these wonderful people, so many of our amazing churches would remain locked and closed to the casual visitor. While our churches may well be full of art treasures and antiques, the real treasures are those people. Long may it continue.

The graffiti surveys have been helped and aided by the involvement of numerous organisations throughout the country. These range from the Marsh Christian Trust, English Heritage, the National Trust, the Heritage Lottery Fund, the Community Archives and Heritage Group and the Council for British Archaeology at one end of the spectrum, down to local groups such as the Waveney Valley Community Archaeology Group, the St Benet's Project, the Binham Local History Group and the Stour Valley Archaeology Group. Particular thanks are due to cathedral archaeologist Roland Harris and the Dean and Chapter of Norwich Cathedral for all their enthusiasm, support and access to this amazing building. There are really too many organisations to mention individually, but all have my heartfelt and sincere thanks.

And then there are the others; the friends, helpers, academics and ne'er-do-wells who have generously offered their time and expertise to give their opinions upon the writing on the walls. To Prof. Sandy Heslop, Dr Jenny Alexander, Becky Williams, Rebecca Hiscott, Jessica Macdonald, Nick Stone, Dr Lorna Richardson, Andrew Macdonald, Frances Barker, Arnold Pacey, Elizabeth McDonald, Heather Hamilton, Sarah Poppy, David Gurney, Dr Karen Smythe, Owen Thompson, Warwick Rodwell, Prof Ronald Hutton, Roger Rosewell, Captain T.M. Lynch, Crystal Hollis, James Wright, Ian Evans, Jackie Hall, C.B. Newham, Robin Stummer, Jennie Hawkes, Dr Julian Litten, Dr John Alban, Sally Badham MBE and, last but by no means least, Timothy Easton – I am eternally grateful. I may not show it all the time, but I am. Particular thanks are due to Jessica Macdonald, who read draft extracts from this work and made numerous corrections, alterations and improvements.

Eternal thanks must go to Rebecca, Alexander and Molly, for all their fantastic support and help – and not screaming aloud (too often) every time I dragged them into a remote church on a sunny afternoon.

The final thanks must go to the one man without whose generosity of spirit and enthusiasm none of this would have happened. Had he not taken the time to show me what he had been working on, to enthuse me with his own drive and determination, then medieval graffiti would really have remained a pretty closed book to us all. And it is to him that I dedicate this small work, in the hope that he can find a use for it as a doorstop or draught excluder. He alone probably understands best just how far we have come, and just how far we have yet to go. I therefore dedicate this book to John Peake of the Blakeney Area Historical Society, who, whether he likes it or not, is the true grandfather of all the modern graffiti surveys.

INDEX

Page numbers in italics denote black and white illustrations

Also of interest:

HOW TO READ A CHURCH

By Richard Taylor

Churches and cathedrals play an essential part in our heritage. As community-centred places of worship and as important tourist attractions, they are visited by millions of people every year. But churches were originally built to be read, and so they are packed with images, symbols and meanings that often need explanation for visitors.

How to Read a Church is a lively and fascinating guide to what a visitor to a church is likely to find there and how to interpret the common images and meanings in church art and architecture – from stained glass windows, to sculptures and building layout. It will explain how to identify people, scenes, details and their significance, and will explore the symbolism of different animals, plants, colours, numbers and letters – and what this all means. It will be an essential guide for anyone who has ever visited or is visiting a church or cathedral, and for those who want to know more about these incredible buildings and the art they contain.

Also of interest:

I NEVER KNEW THAT ABOUT ENGLAND'S COUNTRY CHURCHES

By Christopher Winn

Discover hundreds of facts you never knew about
England's country churches.

Bestselling author Christopher Winn takes us on a
fascinating journey across England in search of hidden
stories, forgotten pasts and secrets that lie within the
nation's country churches. Travel through England and
learn how the churches were host to some of the nation's
biggest events; unearthing the battles fought, won and lost
around them, the births – and deaths – of royalty, the
legends that are laid to rest in the grounds, and the
momentous historical changes that happened with
church spires as their backdrop.

Illustrated throughout with pen and ink drawings,
this book will have you saying time and time again,
'I never knew that!'